How
NOT *to*
Look
FAT

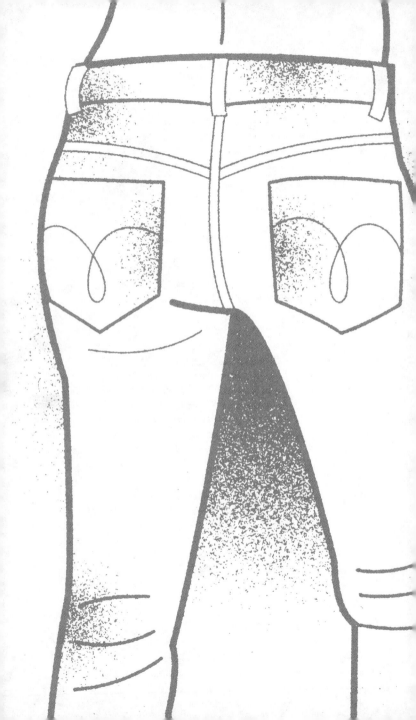

How NOT to Look FAT

Danica Lo

Collins

An Imprint of HarperCollinsPublishers

Illustrations by Vänskap: Rami Niemi, Teemu Väätäinen, Jesse Auersalo, Cajsa Holgersson

HarperCollins books may be purchased for educational, business, or sales promotional use. For information please write: Special Markets Department, HarperCollins Publishers, Inc., 10 East 53rd Street, New York, NY 10022.

FIRST EDITION

Designed by Lorie Pagnozzi

Library of Congress Cataloging-in-Publication Data has been applied for.

ISBN-10: 0-06-089178-5
ISBN-13: 978-0-06-089178-7

06 07 08 09 10   ❖/RRD   10 9 8 7 6 5 4 3 2 1

For my parents,
who have always been
my greatest supporters

TABLE OF CONTENTS

ACKNOWLEDGMENTS

Many thanks to ace agent Melissa Flashman and everyone at Trident Media Group; my brilliant editor Kathryn Huck-Seymour, assistant editor Ryu Spaeth, Shelby Meizlik and Paul Olsewski in publicity, and everyone at Collins.

Deepest gratitude to Faye Penn, who championed my column in the *New York Post;* Libby Callaway, who took a chance on a girl with a faux-hawk; and fabulous photographer Liz Sullivan.

Heartfelt thanks also to Vänskap, my stellar art team—Rami Niemi, Teemu Väätäinen, Jesse Auersalo, and Cajsa Holgersson—for all their patience and hard work.

Thanks also to *How Not to Look Fat* contributors and enthusiasts, including but not limited to: Abe Gurko, Adrienne Denese, Alan Hirsch, Alistair Carr, Allison Hodge, Betty Sze, Brad Zeifman, Brian Long, Carrie Ellen Phillips, Catherine Saxida, Celia Nichols, Charles Stebbens, Cindy Barshop, Cindy Sherwin, Danielle Rosen, Davida Tretout, DeDe Brown, Diane Pernet, Elizabeth Lippman, Emily Listfield, Frederic Fekkai, Gabriel Feliciano, Holly Fussell, Jennifer Cohn, Jennifer DeMarchi, Jennifer Mayer, Jennifer Weinberg, Jonathan Cheban, Julia Murphree, Karen Newman, Kelly Cutrone,

Kelly McKay, Lauren Ramsby, Lisette Sand-Friedman, Liza Bychkov, Melissa Ladines, Melissa Silver, Paula Froelich, Rebecca Beeson, Rex Lott, Rose Fiorentino, Rose Pilato, Sally Blenkey-Tchasova, Sarah Hampton, Sarah Tomczak, Shane Cisneros, Shin at Paul Labrecque, Stephanie Lessing, Stephen Lynch, Steven Cuozzo, and Sydney Foster.

I owe a great deal to my parents, brother, and sister for always being my staunchest supporters.

And Alexander Runne, Aleksi Niemela, Christian Vidal, David Landsel, Eric del Pozo, Farrah Weinstein, Gary Yellowlees, Helen Gim, Jennifer Anderson, Mackenzie Dawson Parks, Maxine Shen, Rob Phillips, Samuel Blake Hofstetter, Sharon Mandler, Tom Jawetz, Tuomas Laitinen, and William Van Meter—whether you realize it or not, without your friendship and support none of this would have been possible.

My name is Danica, and I'm an Oprah addict.

Oprah is a beautiful, brilliant, down-to-earth million-airess who inspires both men and women all over the world every single day. So it was shocking to hear her describe, on national television, how the editor-in-chief of *Vogue* told her she had to lose thirty pounds before appearing on the fashion magazine's cover.

If even Oprah, one of the most influential people in America, is under such unbelievable pressure to have a perfect figure, it's hardly surprising that women every-where feel bad about their bodies.

But I'm not writing this book to preach to you about the importance of self-esteem. (You'll find those manuals in the psychology and self-help section of the bookstore.)

This book is about getting real.

If you've ever spent money on style guides—big, color-ful tomes filled with photographs of sad and happy befores and afters and pictures of clothes that look out-dated six months after you blew $30 on the book—you know that they're probably gathering dust on your shelf at home.

Style is so personal.

I don't want to change your style.

There's one point and one point only to this book. It's a no-holds-barred guide to tips and tricks that will make you look and feel thinner.

Too often, I find, people who write about looking thinner are actually thin. Too often, these writers have never experienced it firsthand.

I've done it. I've cried myself to sleep thinking I'm too fat. I've been hours late to work because I've been paralyzed by my wardrobe—not able to find anything that will fit me in the morning.

I've been the size of the average American woman—14—and I've never managed to dip below a size 10 in my entire adult life. I'm normal. I know I'm normal, but still, like most women, I can't shake the feeling that I'm far too big.

One of the biggest turning points in my body-consciousness was on the very first job I had working as a plus-size model. Not only was I incredibly nervous about the photo shoot, but when I arrived on the job they informed me that I would have to be naked on set (so they could shoot my back).

It was do or die.

So I did.

And I realized that whatever I think about my body and no matter how much I talk myself into a tizzy about my chubbiness, in the end, my body is my body. And that's all there is to it.

See, your body is something you have to carry around with you. You can't just leave it at home. Everyone can see you when you go outside.

So, sure, if you're keen on diet and exercise, that's cool. But you can't change your physique overnight.

And, in the end, it doesn't really matter how you feel your body looks. Because it's all about perception.

I believe there's someone beautiful inside every single woman, even though sometimes the world—and the woman herself—can't see it. The first things so many of us see when we look in the mirror are hips, ass, flab, and rolls. But can you look beyond that and see what's beautiful? That's the first step—the biggest hurdle before beginning to look and feel better.

Ever since my "How Not to Look Fat" column first appeared in the *New York Post,* people approach me all the time for advice—I've helped photograph college facebook photos and on-line profile pictures, and I've set people straight on shopping trips. Lately I've taken to makeover-ambushing my friends.

So many gorgeous girls and women I know unnecessarily feel bad about themselves. But after just a few tips from this book and a couple of waves of the hair and makeup brush, they can hardly believe their eyes.

"That doesn't even look like me!" they say when I show them their "after" snapshots.

"Please," I tell them, "That *is* what you look like. That's you. You're gorgeous. Deal with it."

This book just might change your life.

INTRODUCTION

Whether you're a size 6 or a size 16, everyone has fat days. Maybe you haven't exercised in years, or maybe you had too much salt for dinner last night. If you've ever woken up feeling the bloat—or the fat, as the case may be—this book is for you.

Starting here, follow me on the everywoman quest to look as thin as possible—without breaking a sweat. Because, let's face it, while going to the gym is good for you, for many people it's both time-wise and financially an unaffordable luxury.

Workouts take time and diets fail. Truth is, the most reliable way to look thinner is, well, illusion. Yup, the old smoke and mirrors.

Fact: There are activities already built into daily life—like sleeping, dressing, styling your hair, and applying makeup—that most people do not use to the best of their skinnifying potentials.

This book's motto? You're gorgeous just the way you are. But it can't hurt to learn a few quick tricks.

No tiptoeing on eggshells here—Fat isn't a four-letter word. Eat whatever you want; I'm not here to preach to you about protein percentages. You can be happy, living a full life that includes fats, carbs, and delicious foods. And you still can look fabulous.

Above all: Don't take yourself too seriously.

Let's get started.

Part One Put It On

Changing clothes is the most obvious and the easiest way to make yourself look and feel thinner instantly.

The right neckline, a different length sleeve, or a simple underwear-swap can make a five-, ten-, even fifteen-pound difference in the way you feel, the way you carry yourself, and the way others see you.

From underwear to headscarves, we've got it all covered.

Chapter 1

UNDERWEAR

*F*irst things first.

To build a good anything—be it a home, a sofa, a face full of makeup, or even an argument—you'll need a good foundation. Laying a solid foundation for a top-to-toe slimming look is far easier in some seasons than others. Take summer, which is the most brutally fat season of the year. Soaring temperatures and stifling humidity bring with them grin-and-bare-it hot-weather wardrobe staples like sleeveless tees and skimpy shorts. There's hardly any hope of hiding anything at all behind those strips of fabric otherwise known as sundresses.

But during the rest of the year, when the weather is cooler and there's less chance of sweating to death in more substantial clothing, it's time to think about camouflaging that summer backyard-barbecue-baby around your waist with some good old granny panties.

Just for you, I tried on dozens of pairs of waist-cinching, thigh-slimming, butt-containing, body-shaping underwear. After standing, wriggling, measuring, and almost passing out from the circulation-stunting compression of these garments, I have good news:

Expensive doesn't necessarily equal effective.

There are lots of great bum-belly-blubber-cinching under-things for every budget.

TIP 1: Underwear shopping should be approached in the spirit of ER triage. Before you shop, prioritize. What bothers you the most? What do you consider your problem areas? Hips? Back? Be honest with yourself and take mental notes. Look for undergarments that target these particular issues.

TIP 2: Try it on—While most women only tote bras into the fitting room, don't be shy of trying on undies as well. Keep your own panties on (for hygiene's sake), and shimmy into those grannies. Think about how they feel—can you imagine wearing them all day? Do they cut into your skin?

TIP 3: Consider your toosh. Even though you usually don't have to look at your backside, other people do. A sexy backside is different things to different people, but things like perkiness, smoothness, and curviness are general, universal must-haves.

TIP 4: Test-drive for lumps. Bring a thin-fabric T-shirt or dress to put on over the underwear to see what it looks like under clothing. Consider buying a maximum-coverage piece—one that stretches from just below the bust to the knees—for the sake of minimizing lumpiness at the seams.

TIP 5: Try on more than one brand. Even if you can afford a $50 waist-cincher, it doesn't mean you should eschew all the $10 ones! You'll be surprised at how some cheaper pieces can work just as well, or even better, than their more expensive counterparts.

Don't wear obviously-there underwear. VPL—visible panty lines—and lumpy hips will always make you look chubbier than you are.

At the very height of fashion and luxury, you'll find the incomparable couture corsets made by the 18-inch-waisted Mr. Pearl (nee Mark Pullin), whose work has graced Parisian catwalks and countless celebrity midsections. At his atelier located behind Notre Dame in Paris, Mr. Pearl painstakingly hand-makes elaborate corsets for fashion houses like Dior and his wealthy clients—women like Kylie Minogue, Jerry Hall, and Victoria "Posh Spice" Beckham.

No Lumps!!! ☑

Not keen on compression? Look for a wide waistband with a lot of give.
Hanky Panky panties are one-size-fits-most and they boast a wide lace
waistband that doesn't pinch—this prevents hip bumps and panty lines.
At about $20 a pop, Hanky Pankies are the original best, but not the
cheapest. Lots of other brands are now copying this gimmick, so look
for those wide lace bands at your local panty supplier.

On the other end of the spectrum, Hanes Body
Enhancer maximum control underwear, which resembles
thick pantyhose, is super-smooth and compresses your
waist and hips by up to 1.5 inches all around. It's easy to

EXPERT TIP: "To achieve that ultra slim look,
get in touch with Mr. Pearl, the world-renowned
corsetier—think 15" waists!—and have a couture
corset made. Then you can eat as many cakes
as you like—just lace the corset a bit tighter
after each bite."
—Alistair Carr, fashion designer

wear under nearly anything, comfortable enough to wear all day, and, the best part is, it can be found at drugstores everywhere for under $15—it's a great flab-emergency product. Just watch out for your rear view in these—while this underwear certainly won't flatten or mush your butt, it doesn't do much to shape or flatter it either.

Somewhere in the middle-of-the-road price range is JCPenney's firm control high-waisted thigh slimmer, which costs under $30. This was the most comfortable pair I tried, but that, in turn, means they're not as aesthetically effective. While they left me looking like I had the best butt in town, there was minor lumpiness around my

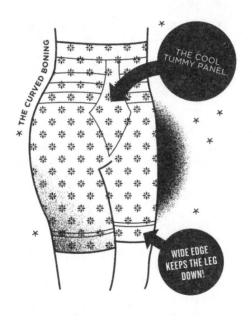

THE COOL TUMMY PANEL.

* THE CURVED BONING

WIDE EDGE KEEPS THE LEG DOWN!

Don't fix what ain't broken: Old-fashioned Rago Shapewear has been sucking in American tummies for over five decades with its smoothing stretch lace and strategically placed paneling and boning.

hips, since they're less constrictive. If you're planning on wearing the undies all day long, JCPenney's are a good choice.

Of course, control-top underwear has been around forever, and if one particular product has worked for over five decades, why fix what ain't broken? That's the philosophy behind old-school all-American company Rago Shapewear, manufacturers of bodyslimmers since the 1950s. Their high-waisted long leg shaper shrank me by an inch all around, and its contoured boning in key areas—like around the hips and lower tummy—minimizes problem spots. They've also, thoughtfully, made the lace hem at the leg adequately wide and stretchy, so there are no weird indentations at the leg-underwear interface. Rago also gets points for the best rear view—firmer, tighter, and ever-so-slightly perkier.

Chapter 2
TOPS

*R*emember when you were a kid and could, on a whim, throw on a T-shirt and shorts to run out and play? Well, those days are over—and they have been since the moment you first sprouted boobs. (If you're flat, don't worry—carry on wearing normal T-shirts; just make sure the shoulders fit and the trunk is body-skimming.)

Here's the skinny on tops: No matter what shape you're in, the top you choose to grace your torso can make or break your look. Now that you're all grown up, don't get caught out in a boxy, shapeless tee. Concert and novelty shirts are fun memorabilia, but the way most of them hang straight off the largest part of your chest will obscure any hint of your womanly figure and waistline.

Don't even get me started on oversized tees.

As a rule, the most flattering top you can buy is a solid-colored deep-V-neck, three-quarter sleeve, slightly stretchy fine-gauge knit that skims your figure and ends right at the top of your hip.

Since most of us like to have more than one kind of top in our closets—variety, spice of life, blah, blah—I've rounded up a list of elements that can help make shopping for slimming tops a bit easier.

NECKLINES: The most flattering necklines come in a V-shape. The V draws attention to your cleavage and the center of your torso—i.e., away from your width.

Rule to live by: The broader and bigger your chest and shoulders, the less fabric you ought to have at your neckline.

For example, if you're busty, don't wear turtlenecks—if your neck is cold, try a scarf instead. If you're less busty, higher-cut necklines tend to be just fine.

Really, though, crewnecks do nothing for anyone's figure—but while they're neutral on a modest-sized chest, they're lethal over larger busts. And, while boatnecks may emphasize your slim collarbone, for anyone who boasts anything over a C cup, a high and wide neckline will only make your shoulders seem broader.

SLEEVE LENGTH: Three-quarter-length sleeves are, absolutely, the most slimming and arm-elongating sleeve length. Period.

Sleeves that are too long add extra fabric and weight to the middle and hip area of your body. Lately more and more contemporary and streetwear labels have been designing tops with ultra-long sleeves—some even feature holes to loop over your thumbs. While these are super-cute (and knuckle-length sleeves make your fingers look really long), unless you're tall and have extra-long legs to counterbalance these extra-long sleeves, your best bet would be to leave this look to the skinny teenagers for whom they're meant.

TRUNK LENGTH: For both short and long torsos, the safest and most flattering hem is one that ends right at the hip. Unless you're ultra-slender, avoid tops that end right at your waist—they'll make you seem short-waisted and larger-of-buttock.

Short, cropped jackets look terrific on smaller-busted, slender-waisted women. But if you are particularly short-waisted, try a longer chemise-length top that ends mid-butt.

Bonus: Mid-butt-length tops make your butt look perkier!

FABRIC: Jersey is not your friend.

Rule to live by: The softer the flesh, the chunkier the fabric should be—knits, wovens, any fabric.

Not only will a heavier fabric have less of a chance of actually being caught between folds of flesh, but the way a fabric like six-ply cashmere—substantial, but still thin—softly, gracefully glides over womanly curves is absolutely, undeniably a beautiful thing.

And besides, ever see a really chubby person in some super-thin T-shirt fabric?

Yeah, it's not pretty.

Don't be that person.

Dictionary of Necklines

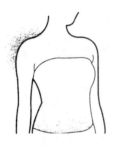

Strapless tops (like bandeaus and tubes) are good for most women who don't need the support of bra straps. Not needing a bra means this: no sagging—from a side view, your nipple should sit approximately halfway between your shoulder and your elbow. A potential pitfall: If you have a bad case of back fat or bad posture, a tube top is not for you.

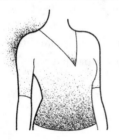

V-necks are the safest bet and are flattering on the vast majority of women.

Boatnecks are great on small to moderate busts, but should be avoided by broad-shouldered babes.

Simple shirt collars generally are flattering, but even more so when flipped up—French women, New England prepsters, and Usher do it all the time. Popping your collar enlongates the neck and casts a flattering shadow along your jawline.

Mandarin collars are most flattering on smaller-boned women with narrow shoulders and smaller busts.

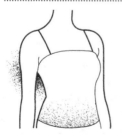

Spaghetti-strapped tank tops should be body-skimming from just below the bust downward—any top that hangs loose from the widest part of your chest will obscure your waist.

Tops

Mock turtlenecks aren't flattering. Period.

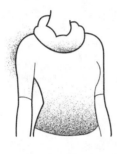

Cowl-necks are gorgeous on slender figures, but unflattering on thicker torsos and over big chests.

Stand-up collars look brilliant on nearly everyone—the bigger your chest, the bigger your collar ought to be. But, don't go overboard. I have big boobs and will tend to opt for V-necks over collars.

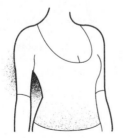

Scoop necks are better on small to moderate chests, as the roundness of the scoop may have the tendency to overemphasize the roundness of the buxom bosom.

BACK FAT

In the wide world of adipose tissue, there are some deposits that simply are more favorable than others.

Busty? Good.

Booty? Good.

Back fat? Eh, not so good.

Sad fact: A lumpy back is almost as unavoidable as cellulite.

Unless you're model-thin, you're probably afflicted with back rolls—you know, those unattractive bulges that make you look like a stuffed sausage in what was meant to be a tight, sexy shirt.

Sure, you could go running five times a week and wedge yourself into a Nautilus contraption to press-up, pull-down, crunch, and tighten your muscles. But that's the hard way.

Here are five quick-and-easy, tried-and-true ways to reduce the appearance of those mini-rolls.

TIP 1: STAND UP STRAIGHT

Good posture is cheaper than liposuction.

Informal polls indicate that standing up straight can make you look up to fifteen pounds lighter—and your back more than 50 percent smoother!

To see what good posture can do for you, try this in front of a mirror (or a friend; or your mother, for honesty): stand up against a wall, squeeze your shoulders up as close to your ears as you can, hold for a second, then drop them. This is the position your shoulders *should* be in.

Voila! You're skinny!

TIP 2: ALL HERALD THE UNDERSHIRT REVIVAL

Flashback to prepubescence—right now there are loads of gorgeous camisoles and undershirts in stores just waiting to be taken home.

Perfect for layering, undershirts of all sorts give your clothes something else (i.e., not your back fat) to cling to. The same principle applies to long slips.

Smooth fabrics—like silk, satin, and, my personal favorite, easy-care polyester—in a body-skimming, not body-clinging, shape work best to minimize friction.

TIP 3: KNITS, NOT JERSEY

Some of the biggest fashion disasters happen in jersey—that thin, clingy, unforgiving fabric.

No matter how attractive, comfortable, cheap, or machine-washable a basic jersey top or dress may seem, this garment is just not for everybody—but who ever said that fashion is democratic?

To camouflage back rolls, step away from the jersey and head straight for the knits. From cashmere to cotton to merino to viscose, knits are just as versatile and wearable—and, because of their thicker texture, less revealing and, ergo, more forgiving.

TIP 4: SUPPORT YOURSELF

You can suck in your gut, but you can't suck in your back—so let support undergarments do it for you. There are waist cinchers out there that specifically target the area between your bust and your hips, leaving you with a smoother side and rear view.

If you're not too keen on corsetry, a mid-torso-length sports bra under a tight shirt also does the trick. Wear it over your regular bra for better shape, lift, and separation—and to avoid the dreaded uni-boob.

TIP 5: IF YOU CAN'T HIDE IT, DECORATE IT

Finally, if you've tried everything and still aren't satisfied with your rear view, throw on a cute little capelet or shawl. This piece of clothing will, literally, camouflage any lumps that may remain. Look for lightweight, crocheted sparkly or beaded ones that catch the light and distract the eye. The best length? Aim for one that ends midway between your bust and your belly button—it will make your waist look super-slim. And skip the heavy shawls—wearing a big woolly cape indoors makes you look (a) fatter and (b) foolish.

Foolproof Tip: Wear a bra that doesn't ride up in the back and choose a moderately heavy cashmere cable-knit hip-length body-skimming sweater. Rule of thumb? The bigger the back fat, the chunkier the cables.

Chapter 3

JEANS

Shopping for jeans is like trying to find Mr. Right—a totally aggravating, exhausting, and depressing experience.

No matter how many pairs I lug into the fitting room and no matter how much I sweat and how many tears I shed while sucking in my tummy and hoping for a flattering fit, I'm always left wondering: If jeans are supposed to be a basic, why is finding the right pair so profoundly difficult?

Maybe there's just too much to choose from. These days, the denim market is a heaving industry worth billions, so it's no surprise that everyone who owns a sewing machine is jumping on the jeans bandwagon.

In the past few years, there has been an even greater boom in the denim sector. There is a host of new and slimming shapes, cuts, fades, and dyes on the market—jeans companies are going all out with both high-tech innovations, like built-in cellulite-busting technology, and high-design concepts, like creative stitching that lifts and shapes the toosh.

Choosing the right pair of jeans is, ultimately, a very personal decision.

For example, I'm a huge fan of Earnest Sewn's Hefner jeans because their waistband dips slightly in the front, creating a more flattering waistline, and Levi's Premium Ultimate Boot Cuts because they're not insanely long, feature slimming fading down the front of the thighs, and aren't too designer-jeans-victim-y.

However, my pear-shaped style-writer friend swears by Salt Works and Kasil jeans because they're super-flattering on her petite, small-waisted, bootylicious frame.

So, sorry to say, you're going to have to do your own rounds in the fitting room, but to ease your search, here are some basic principles that might help you on your way.

COLOR: While darker denims are inherently more slimming, they're not always fashionable. No matter what shade of blue or black you fancy, watch out for broad horizontal bleaching across places like the butt and the pelvis.

The lighter the color, the more that part of your body will stand out, so make sure the color gradations are flattering. Long vertical bits down the center of the thighs is a good bet.

The inexplicable world of designer denim: I've taken an informal poll among my friends and none of us can figure out why, these days, jeans are so damn long. In fact, they're so damn long that I and everyone else I know always have to get jeans cut or hemmed.

Notice, though, that after jeans are shortened, the whiskers (those horizontal bleached stripes around your pelvis and in the backs of your knees) and some fading

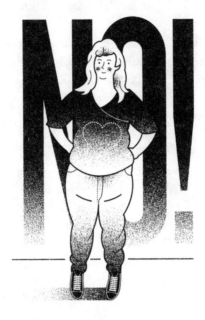

Fat 911! Mom jeans (à la *Saturday Night Live*)—those high-waisted, tapered, poofy-topped jeans that exacerbate all the problem parts you, um, love so much. Tip: avoid pleats, tapered legs, high cinched waists, and extra butt fabric.

(like on the knees or behind the thighs) just aren't in the right place anymore.

The once chic back-of-the-knee lighter bits now hang down in the middle of your calf and the pale front-of-thigh parts practically graze your ankles.

It's like you've somehow sunk into the ground.

This is no good. Looking stumpy is never good.

So watch out for this when you're trying on jeans and think about how short you'll have them hemmed—especially if you're buying fancy $200 jeans, whose makers think that all their customers are six-feet-tall models.

HOW NOT TO LOOK FAT

Good back pocket placement is key to a flattering rear view. Pockets that are angled away from the center seam make your butt look much wider than it is.

Jeans

The more parallel the inner edges of the pockets are to the middle seam, the better your butt will look.

HOW NOT TO LOOK FAT

Blue Cult, a celeb-favorite jeans label, makes world-famous Butt Lifter jeans. The back pockets are slightly raised, and there are magic seams above each cheek that make your rear look like two perfect, perky peaches.

Jeans

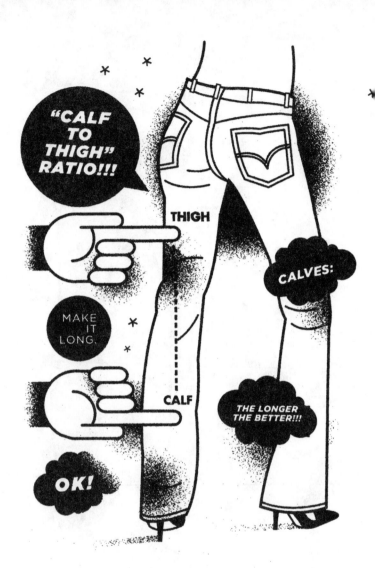

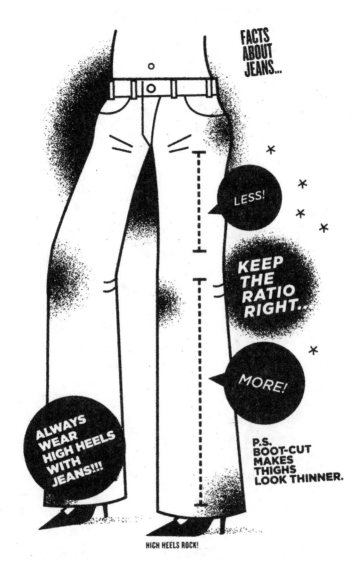

Even though it may seem counterintuitive at first, the fact is that the most flattering jeans are those where the calf is wider and longer than the thigh. Choose boot-cut jeans for everyday wear—bell-bottoms are fun, but too dramarama if they're not the trend du jour (they can also make you look shorter than you really are).

Jeans

Chapter 4
PANTS

*T*rousers, slacks, dungarees—no matter what funny name you give them, pants nowadays, far more than skirts, are what American women live in on a day-to-day basis.

But just as everyone's got their favorite pair—mine are black Helmut Lang tuxedo trousers I bought years ago that, even my mother concedes, make me look thin—everyone's also got some major pants problems hiding in their collections.

With so many styles to choose from, the temptation to stock up on unflattering styles of this indispensable wardrobe staple leads many women to fill their closets with tons of badly chosen bottoms—all for the sake of variety.

But here's a bit of advice: **Variety's not all it's chalked up to be.**

Ever notice how real fashion people—industry icons like Giorgio Armani, Donna Karan, and Karl Lagerfeld—always look basically the same?

It doesn't matter what's in style and what season it is.

They don't give a flying hoot if Russian cassock is the look of the year. Sod the peasant shirt and never mind the bollocks—they're sticking to their guns and flying the flag for monotony.

They've found their look; they've found what works for them; they know what they like.

Not only does finding your true fashion self make getting dressed in the morning a piece of cake, but having a signature look shows that an individual has a point of view—she knows herself, she knows what looks good, and she's not desperately grasping at trends.

That said, to put it to practical use, here's my advice: If you find pants that make you look hot, buy more than one pair. Buy, like, five. Good pants are hard to find. And anyway, who cares if they're all the same if you wind up with five pairs of pants that make you look hot?

If you haven't yet found the trousers of your dreams, don't panic. Shopping for pants is a lot like shopping for jeans—real tough, but super-rewarding in the end. Follow the same principles of proportion and color as you do with denim—i.e., look for a dark color boot-cut with a longer, wider calf proportion.

Vertical patterns, like pinstripes, lengthen the leg and tend to be very flattering. Try to avoid any patterns that are round, square, or that run horizontally—at best they're harmless, but, for the most part, they're horrible.

Unless you're a model being paid to strut down a (specifically) Paris runway, stay away from high-waisted styles, pleats, and tapered trousers in light colors. Just remember that while you may covet the supermodel look, it is the supermodel look and (I'm going to take a wild stab and guess that) you are probably not a supermodel.

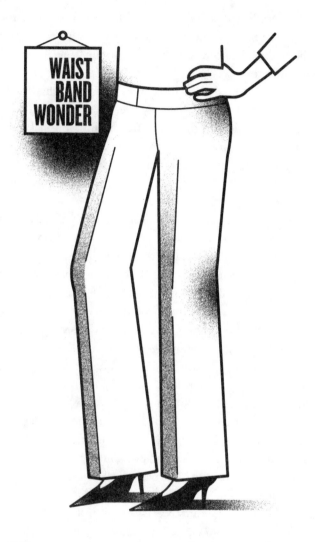

WAISTBAND: Look for a mid-rise style that's high enough to cover the lower abdomen, but low enough to see the side curvature of your waist. A wider waistband—think 3 inches plus—not only helps to rein in the tummy but also makes your butt look smaller from the back.

OBJECTS IN THE REAR VIEW MAY BE LARGER THAN THEY APPEAR: Improving your rear view is all about visually reducing the amount of fabric that seems to be devoted to the general badonkadonk area. A wider waistband defines the upper parameter, but what about the lower?

Unfortunately, since most dressier pants don't have externally stitched pockets to delineate the borders of your butt space, you're left relying on the interaction between center seam and the waistband for lifting and sculpting illusions.

Make sure to check out your back view in the fitting room mirror.

In the case of trousers, I find that unless there are back pockets, a non-clinging material like gabardine, which doesn't cup your buttocks and, instead, hangs straight down from the center of your butt, yields a far more flattering rear view than any butt-clinging stretchy textile.

CREASES: You already know that pleats are the work of devil's spawn, but creases are like an angel singing. A clean, knife-sharp crisp crease straight down the front of each leg is terrific in suiting trousers—the vertical line works wonders for elongating and slimming the leg.

ALWAYS: Wear heels with pants. Heels make your legs look longer.

Chapter 5

SKIRTS AND SHORTS

One of the greatest life lessons I've ever learned is that no matter how much you want something, no matter how much you wish for something, if you're not meant to have it, you can't have it.

This is the reason why:
(1) I did not go to medical school,
(2) I have not won the lottery, and
(3) I do not look that good in pants.

I have a body for skirts. I guess that's just by default, since I don't have the body for pants. Some people have the body for both, but I am not one of those people.

Truth is: Some people just don't look very good in pants. If you are one of these people, you either can lament this fact, fight it your whole life, and go on looking bad while wearing pants, or you can throw up your hands, deal with it, and put on a skirt.

I say: **Work with what you've got.**

What's the skirt-resistance movement all about anyway? Skirts are much cuter than pants, and they come in tons of flattering shapes and lengths.

Here are my best tips for finding one that will work for you:

LONG SKIRTS: Long skirts look better in drapey, clingy fabrics—like the evil jersey. If you can't wear drapey, clingy fabrics (which is a statement that applies to most of us), then you probably shouldn't be wearing a long skirt.

If you choose a long skirt made of a stiffer, less drapey fabric, you're just going to wind up looking like a tent (in an A-line skirt) or a nun (in a straight skirt). I mean, when you boil it down to its essence, a long skirt really is just a small tarp.

If, indeed, you go against my advice and choose a long skirt anyway, for heaven's sake, please don't wear one that's covered in flowers.

CALF-LENGTH SKIRTS: Avoid.

Alright, if you absolutely insist on wearing one, try to find one that ends somewhere above the fattest part of your calf—like right below your knee. If you must go longer (maybe for religious purposes), pick a hem that hits at the midpoint between the fattest part of your calf and your ankle. Whatever you do, don't pick a skirt that ends dead-center at the widest part of your calf.

In fact, **never pick anything that ends at the fattest part of anything on your body.** For example, if you have a thick waist, don't pick a top that ends dead at your waist. If you have fat ankles, don't pick ankle straps or boots that end right in the middle of your fat ankles.

Doing that makes the perceiver's eye believe everything it can't see is at least as wide as that endpoint. Hems that end at strategically curved and slim points on your body are far more flattering.

Let's take this principle and apply it to:

KNEE-LENGTH SKIRTS: Get one that ends right above the knee or right at the knee (two of the slimmest points on your leg). Below the knee is okay if the skirt is very fitted—like a pencil skirt.

As for those poofy '50s-style skirts that go in and out of style every two years? Yeah, I love those too, but you better not go near them unless you're slender of torso. Since they are so voluminous, the best way to counterbalance them is with an ultra-slender top.

Think back to all the period costume drama movies you've seen where the ladies are wearing enormous skirts. The actresses who look best in those dresses were definitely the ones with itsy-bitsy boobs.

MINISKIRTS: Look at your thighs.

I want you to take a good, honest look at your thighs. A lot of you aren't going to like what you see. But, if you're lucky, you might be able to find a slight concave curve on your inner thigh. If you're really lucky, there will actually be a gap between your thighs when you're standing with your feet together.

If not, don't feel bad, it's really not a big deal—the gap just serves as a useful guideline for picking out the right length miniskirt.

Anyway, right there, anywhere from the middle of that curve to near the top of that curve is where your miniskirt

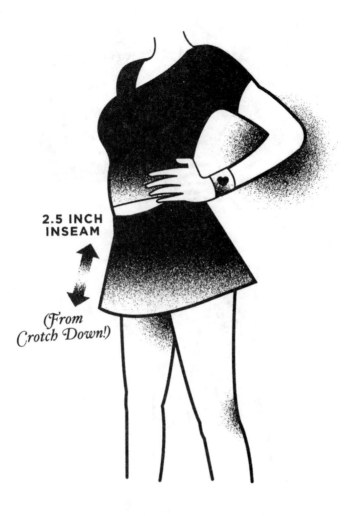

2.5 INCH INSEAM

(From Crotch Down!)

should end. If you don't happen to have the curve, you probably shouldn't be wearing a miniskirt. However, I won't stop you, so if you insist, pick a skirt that ends somewhere between two and a half to four inches from your crotch. That would be the most flattering length.

The same principles that apply to miniskirts also apply to shorts—look for a 2.5-inch inseam that ends near the top of your inner-thigh curvature—except that with shorts, if you don't have that gap between your thighs, I would really, strongly, emphatically recommend you do yourself a favor and don't wear shorts at all.

If you are a normal person and your thighs touch, then your shorts will ride up when you walk. You will wind up with lots of fabric bunched up in your crotch. Listen, I'm just tellin' it like it is. A bunch of fabric stuck in your crotch is neither pretty nor comfortable.

TOP-HEAVY CHEAT SHEET

EXPERT TIP: "Never underestimate the power of standing up straight, or thinking that you are taller than you are."
—Carrie Ellen Phillips, fashion publicist

You know you're top-heavy when:
(1) Your boobs are bigger than your badonkadonk,
(2) You look down and can't see your feet for the hills, or
(3) You can fit one of your bra cups over your head. Like a beanie.

UNDERWEAR: Getting the right size bra is the most important thing you can do for your figure. Low-hanging udders are not a good look.

"Bra, schma," you, and many others, may say to me.

No, really, the right bra will change your life. It will also prevent your breast tissue from sagging in the future.

Here is how to check your bra for fit:
(1) Your nipples are supposed to sit on or about the midpoint between your shoulder and your elbow level.
(2) The center of your bra should lie flat against your chest—not floating in midair or pointing outward.
(3) You shouldn't be experiencing any four-boob-effect squishing. If you are, try a bigger cup size.
(4) The back of your bra band should not be riding up over the course of the day. If it is, try a smaller bra band.

In Atlanta and New York, the best place to get measured is at the specialty lingerie store Intimacy. I've been measured all over the world—everywhere I've ever bought bras—and in America, Intimacy does the best job. Unfortunately, since they're so good at what they do, there's often upward of an hour wait for a fitting appointment.

Since bra-size measuring isn't an exact science, I wouldn't recommend trying to suss out your own size at home. The best thing to do is to head to your closest, largest lingerie department and try on a variety of sizes until you find the right bra for you. And, just like control-top underwear, don't forget to bring a thin-fabric tee with you so you can see how the undergarments look under clothes.

HAIR: Don't get big hair! You'll wind up looking like Dolly Parton. Yes, I love Dolly too, but few people can pull off walking around all day every day looking like her.

"But Pamela Anderson has big hair," you say. "And I wouldn't mind looking like her."

To that I say: "Pamela Anderson is insanely thin. If you have Pamela Anderson's body, what are you doing reading this book? You should be at the salon getting big hair instead."

And stay away from pixie cuts too (which really only look good on birdlike people like Mia Farrow).

TOPS: Definitely a V-neck, no question about it. Big-breasted women also tend to look short-waisted, so a hip-length top is ideal for elongating the torso.

BAGS: Pick a tote or a clutch that you can carry. Wedging a bag under your shoulder, right by the biggest part of your body, certainly won't help balance out your proportions.

PANTS: You can wear almost any kind of pant you want—just not baggy, loose ones! Wearing loose pants technically may balance out your proportions—magazines tell you this all the time—but they make you look fat from head to toe! Why would you want to expand your bottom half to be just as big as the biggest part of your body? No, no, no.

SHOES: Depending on how tall you are, you may or may not be able to get away with wearing flats. To be safe, if you're shorter than 5′6″, wear at least a 2-inch heel. The risk with being big-boobed is that everyone else who is taller than you will look downward at you and only see boobs. Rising to the occasion, in heels, will make you seem less booby overall.

ACCESSORIES MADE FOR YOU: Wristbands and bracelets; hip-slung belts.

Chapter 6
ONESIES

*O*ne-piece dressing is like frozen dinners—a godsend on harried weekdays. No need to mix and match—throwing on a dress or jumpsuit is a quick fix on those mornings you can barely drag your sorry self out of bed to the closet door.

Yes, I said "jumpsuit."

JUMPSUITS: Are great and, believe it, really flattering. A few years ago, avant garde design collective Bless went so far as to devise a full-on suit-shirt-tie one-piece jumpsuit combo that was pull-on-and-go—as in, the suit, shirt, and tie were all sewn together.

Take a cue from Bless—the best jumpsuits are tailored. Look for simple, solid colors and make sure the shoulders fit like a glove—the entire jumpsuit will hang off those shoulders (like the way your entire face hangs off your cheekbones), so they have to be perfect.

While I prefer mine ultra-tailored, slightly '80s (Thierry Mugler made amazing ones—I got mine on eBay), with hidden zips, some recent military-inspired jumpsuits have "feature" metallic buttons that draw attention to the center of the body and the shoulders—all very good places for people to be looking. (I mean, obviously, don't buy things that have "feature" buttons haphazardly scattered around on the stomach or the butt.)

DRESSES: The most universally flattering dresses on the market are simple black sheath dresses—they're so chic, so Audrey Hepburn. Since sheath dresses are slightly, but not oppressively, tailored, they're body-skimming, sleek, and perfect for nearly every occasion. Other slimming colors and patterns, besides the obvious black, include navy, any deeper solid color you may be comfortable with, and pinstripes.

For a curvier look, or if you're more top-heavy, choose a drop-waist halter dress—department stores stock up on them in the spring and summer. The dropped waist elongates the torso while the halter silhouette will make you look like a perfect hourglass.

TOP TIP: When layering a cardigan or a jacket over a dress, make sure your underlayer is darker than your overlayer—this color contrast will make your body seem to sink back, away from the outer layer, and, as a result, you will look slimmer.

The simple sheath dress made with a bit of stretch (so the fabric moves with you) is the perfect wardrobe staple. It's easy to find at every price range, and the shape can be tweaked and accessorized to compensate for your personal body neuroses—for example, if you are concerned about your armpits, you can find a cap-sleeve sheath dress; if you want to cover your stomach, put on a cardigan.

HOW NOT TO LOOK FAT

DESIGNER CHEAT SHEET FOR LADIES SIZE 14+

If you're tired of shopping the same old plus-size departments and boutiques and you have money to splurge, you may be surprised to know that many of the world's top designers make clothes in sizes beyond size 6.

Christian Dior sizes some boutique items up to 18, which I didn't know until I accidentally bought a size 18 black wrap top from Dior a few years ago. (Note: It's machine washable and doesn't need ironing—best purchase ever!)

Legendary Japanese designer Yohji Yamamoto doesn't just make fancy sweats for Adidas (under the Y-3 moniker). His own two lines, Yohji Yamamoto and Y's, are brilliant sources of generously cut, extraordinarily well-made classic and fashion-driven clothing for all sizes and shapes.

Yves Saint Laurent boutiques can order their luxurious and iconic Parisian fashions in up to a size 16. And a few seasons back I bought a size 14 stretch Versace gown that easily could have fit a bigger girl than I.

Comme des Garçons, designed by avant garde legend Rei Kawakubo, is also especially generous in sizing—if something "small" from Comme fits me, I think it's quite promising for the other normal-size women of the world!

As for you ladies who lunch (and really do eat at lunch), Chanel suits size up to a 46, which is about a size 14 to 16. However, one fabulous fashionista in the know told me that there are two extra inches of fabric squirreled away inside every suit seam, so the potential to take the garment out to up to a size 50 is there. And a 50 is about an 18 to 20 in America!

The best part is that since most people don't know these sizes are available at all, you'll find a lot of pieces left over at the end of the season in discount stores (like New York's famous Century 21) and in outlet centers all around the world. (I mean, did you really think I was paying retail??)

*I*n my senior year of college, something must have hit me on the head, because for about a minute I thought I'd be climbing the corporate ladder after graduation. In retrospect, maybe I never made it onto even Rung One because I couldn't get over the mental hurdle of having to wear a suit to work ... ever. (That, and, to this day, despite having piles of them as friends, I don't really know what investment bankers do.)

Now, years later and far from the financial world, I've had time to suss out the principles of the perfect suit. And while wearing one day-in and day-out isn't the funnest form of professional attire (my freshman year roommate wins that one—she played Boo Boo at Jellystone National Park), it certainly can be bearable, flattering, and, dare I say, sexy.

The most important things to avoid when buying a suit are excessive accoutrements—embroidery, flashy buttons, crazy contrasting appliqués, etc. Also, even if they're extra-comfy and super-cheap, stay away from those loose-fitting synthetic pantsuits that become fashionable every five to seven years. Sure, they're comfortable and they're probably easy-care polyester, but they're the sweatsuit of corporate dressing. And you wouldn't wear sweatpants to work, would you?

Instead of loose-fitting, **find comfort in a good fit.**

Single-breasted suits generally are more slimming. Forget double-breasted—overlaying fabric and two rows of

SUPER-STRUCTURED SHOULDERS.

MEDIUM LAPEL.

SINGLE-BREASTED.

HIP LENGTH.

The Perfect Suit.

KNEE-LENGTH PENCIL SKIRT.

buttons over a substantial chest or stomach is not going to make anything look smaller. Look for a hip-length jacket and pencil skirt, both of which are professional-looking and timeless and will balance out almost any figure and proportion flaws you think you have.

TOP TIPS: Does the term "shoulder pads" scare you? Reality check: Little shoulder pads are your friends. While draped clothing tends to hang off your boobs (and stomach, and whatever else sticks out), tailored clothing hangs off your shoulders. A wee boost in the shoulder blade department lends a more upright structure to the jacket—it improves the look of your posture, nicely frames your front view, and can, oftentimes, make your butt look smaller by comparison.

Look for: Sharp collars, stand-up collars, and collars rebelliously turned up à la 1950s motorcycle-riding bad boys. Unbuttoned deep-V-neck collars all flipped up make your neck look extra long, minimize your double chin, and draw attention to the center of your body—it's slimming, sassy, and super-sexy.

(Okay, yes, we've already determined that I don't work in the corporate world. I'm sure The Man would prefer it if you kept your collar down during office hours.)

Avoid: Checkered patterns, shiny fabrics like crepe de chine, and ultra-heavy material like tweed.

PEAR-SHAPE CHEAT SHEET

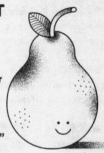

You know you're pear-shaped if:
(1) Your badonkadonk is bigger than your boobs,
(2) You think of leggings as the eighth deadly sin, and
(3) If you were a country, "Bootylicious" would be your national anthem.

UNDERWEAR: Control-top underwear is especially effective on pear-shaped bodies, so check out the chapter on underwear. One of the biggest pitfalls for pear-shaped ladies is picking out butt-flattening underwear and pants.

Just as buxom girls who wear minimizer bras will wind up looking wider and fatter, the wrong bottom-wear can have the same effect. So make sure to check out that rear view, and don't be afraid to try on the undies before you buy!

HAIR: Stay away from pixie cuts, super-tight ponytails, pineapple hair, or slicked-back dos—you don't want to wind up looking like a bowling pin! Aim for a fuller hairstyle to balance out your vertical proportions.

TOPS: If you're not too big-boobed, pick a boatneck top, which is collarbone-flattering and more fabric-substantial on top than a deep-V-neck. Since a boatneck top makes your shoulders look slightly wider and more substantial, it will help balance out your hippier proportions. And if you score a long, mid-hip-length one (try American Apparel, they've got great ones), it will minimize the perceived space devoted to your toosh.

BAG: Pick a shoulder bag instead of a tote. Your goal is to carry the least amount of extra lower-body weight possible.

PANTS: Pick matte, dark, solid-color bottoms for sure—this means no white, florals, or pastels! Lighter colors, crazy patterns, or shiny fabrics will make your rear view stand up and shine like the moon.

SHOES: Please wear heels. Sorry, but your big butt makes your legs look shorter, so you need to do everything you can to diminish this particular side effect of being bootylicious.

ACCESSORIES MADE FOR YOU: Chunky necklaces, cool hats, capelets, shrugs.

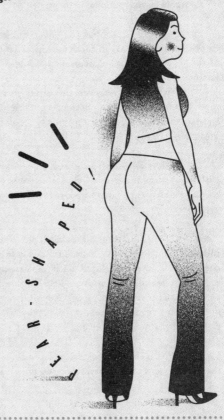

PEAR-SHAPED!

HOW NOT TO LOOK FAT

Chapter 8
SHOES

*C*arrie Bradshaw, you're not alone. Nearly every woman I know is madly, deeply, hopelessly devoted to the pursuit of the perfect shoe.

It's certainly no surprise. Shoes fit you, even on your fat days. And a "feature shoe" can be *the* key element in constructing a stylish outfit. Never mind that footwear can also make or break the proportions of any outfit—and your figure.

The enduringly fashionable high-heel slingback, available in flattering beiges and browns every fall, is incredibly graceful and leg-lengthening—though, truth be told, a smidge officey and boring. On the other hand, wearing a kitten heel, even if it's the trendiest shoe du jour, will make you look like you're so fat that you've squashed your heel down.

Then there is the classic mid-heel D'Orsay pump—possibly the most universally flattering shoe ever designed—worn on the runway and in photo shoots by nearly every model in the '80s and early '90s. These days, D'Orsay pumps are considered more classic, less fashion-fashion shoes and can be found everywhere from your local Payless Shoe Source to the Manolo Blahnik boutique. It's a style that's prevailed because it's flattering.

If your gams happen to be on the slightly less-coltish side, try a chunky or sculpted heel for balance—and to avoid the corndogs-on-sticks look you might get with stilettos.

The basic rule is simple: the chunkier the leg, the chunkier the heel ought to be. It's all about proportions, baby.

It's also all about shunning ankle straps, which "sever" your leg at your ankle. They make your legs look shorter. And we all need shorter legs like we need holes in our heads.

Dictionary of Shoes

Chunky-heel pump: The rule is: The chunkier the leg, the chunkier the heel.

Slingback: In a fleshtone color, this shoe is sexy and slimming.

Stiletto slide: Pick one that's cut lower in front to lengthen your leg line and show off your cute little toesies.

Bad mule: Cut too high, mules have a leg-shortening effect.

UGG boot: The bigger the shoe, the thinner your leg will look.

Good mule: Cut lower, the mule is a graceful, ladylike shoe that won't break up the line of your leg.

Shoes

D'Orsay pump: The ultimate skinny shoe.

Bad Mary Jane: Ankle straps "sever" the leg from the foot and make legs look shorter and wider.

Sculpted heels can enhance the grace of a thick ankle.

Ballet flat: Lower cut is more leg-lengthening and more flattering.

Look for: Nude, fleshtone, or neutral colors will blend better with your skin, your hosiery, or whatever you're wearing to extend your leg line and make your gams look longer.

Pointed toes elongate the foot and, ergo, the leg. Round toes are second best. Stay away from square toes entirely—they make your feet look like blocks.

A chunky, curved heel is a good, safe bet as well. Some of the best and most durable chunky heels come from mid-priced stores like Kenneth Cole and Nine West since, let's face it, rich people have little use for chunky heels. (See, the reason super-expensive shoes tend to have toothpick-width heels is because the women who can afford to blow $1,500 on a pair of pumps don't actually have to walk anywhere if they don't want to.)

For fat feet: If you're going to wear street sneakers, pick Converse. They make your feet look tiny.

Pick your battles: You can pick your battles—big shoes like Terry de Havilland platforms (from the 1960s, but reissued last year—they're a fashion it-girl favorite), Doc Martens, or UGGs make your feet and ankles look huge but your legs look thinner. After all, the bigger the shoe, the thinner your leg.

BOOTS: I've suffered my whole life from a pervasive fear of fall footwear. Since my calves, which measure 15.5 inches around, are bigger than my neck (no joke), I've always thought of myself, pitifully, as a casualty of the boot-making world.

Until last winter.

After spending so many years freezing my big legs off, I'd nearly given up on finding boots that fit. Then, one fateful day, the fashion gods smiled upon me and I found fabulous knee-high boots by Belgian designer Ann Demeulemeester that fit like a glove.

Since then, not only have I become an avid collector of all things Demeulemeester (she makes hats that fit my humongous head too!), but I've been on the hunt for other designer boots that fit larger calves. Cole Haans are pretty darn good too.

Boots are like potato chips. Once you start, you can't have just one.

TOP TIP: Measure your calves around their widest point, then call stores and ask how wide their widest boots are. This will drive sales staff nutso, but will save you hours in the mall.

The widest calf-span I've ever found was a pair of slouchy nappa leather stilettos—they measured eighteen inches around. That's like the size of a cantaloupe! Don't give up people! Big boots are out there!

If you've fallen in love with boots that don't fit, seek out your local cobbler—boots can be stretched as a last resort.

If you're not too keen on the hunt, opt instead for a slightly lower boot—one that ends midcalf. Lace-up boots are adjustable for different calf sizes. And some boots are more sculpted and curvy through the heel, which makes your legs instantly look curvier and sexier, no matter what size they are.

Some great shapes for boots: tall and slouchy; riding boots; slim-fitting ankle-covering boots with sculpted stiletto heels.

SOCKS: For every shoe, there's a sock. Just make sure you can't see it.

Socks that end at your ankles do the same thing ankle straps do—they visually sever your legs at that point. Pick secret socks—ones that hide in your shoes—instead. You can get these everywhere—Gap makes some great ones called "Not Socks"—but if you can't find any, just fold your socks down into your shoes.

FOR YOUR OWN GOOD: Don't wear lace-up ankle boots with skirts. Victorian Shmictorian. Who cares whether it's hot or not—it just looks terrible.

Chapter 9

OUTERWEAR

𝒥ust as I believe in differentiating between "outdoor voices" and "indoor voices," I believe in "outside clothes" and "inside clothes"—so much so that during the summer I become utterly distressed with the weather, the humidity, and the complete impossibility of wearing a jacket.

So naturally, my obsession with outerwear has led me to acquire a wardrobe full of jackets and coats. These naturally bulky items can't be faulted for their chubba factor—after all, they are meant to be big enough to fit comfortably over an entire outfit.

Over the last few years I've found some brilliant and slimming outerwear shapes, styles, and designs that, once mastered, will leave you never wanting to shed your coat again. I love some of my winter coats so much that I often will find an excuse to wear them all day—even indoors!

First things first, though: If you have a barn jacket or anything that resembles a barn jacket, get rid of it. Sometimes, in the fall, which is prime barn jacket season,

I look around and balk at how many grown-up women actually still own boxy, quilted jackets. In college, everyone had a barn jacket. College is not a phase upon which anyone looks back and remarks how chic and fashionable they were. A lot of this can be blamed on the ubiquity of the barn jacket—that boxy, quilted, corduroy-collared brown thing that made you look like a fat farmer. What, are you surprised? It's called a "BARN" jacket, lady. Toss it.

Here are some tips on how to find a non–barn jacket that will work for you:

THE COLLAR: The bigger the coat, the bigger the collar ought to be. That is my rule. This means that if you choose a floor-length coat, it better have a good size collar—otherwise it just won't be proportionally flattering.

Not only is a big collar super-important for proportional balance, but on a coat you can stand up a big collar for warmth and for height. It will make you look taller because, instead of looking like one big ball of insulation, a good size collar will frame your face and emphasize the garment's length and vertical sleekness.

Like on blazers and formal shirts, I recommend pointed, not rounded, collars. This is simply because round = fat.

THE SHOULDERS: Absolutely have to be fitted properly. Just like suits, the entire coat will hang and drape off your shoulders, so it's essential that the shoulders aren't too big. If you purchase your winterwear in early fall, make sure you bring at least a light sweater to try on underneath so you don't wind up with something too small.

THE LENGTH: Outerwear is fun because you have great leeway with length—almost anything (with the odd exception of ankle-length) can be flattering. The rule: The longer the coat, the more fitted it needs to be.

Special Cases

PUFFAS AND PARKAS: Cold-weather sisters, you'll be glad to hear that puffa jackets and parkas are a definite Do. However, they are among the riskiest category of coat, so please be careful to select fitted parkas and puffas that end somewhere between mid-hip and the knee. We've all seen those women in the ankle-length puffy parkas. Don't they look like they're wearing garbage bags, sausages, and/or poop?

In lieu of a collar, pick a parka with a fabulous "feature" hood, like a fur trim or in a special shape that will draw attention to your face and the top of the jacket—anything that drags and weights your gaze downward will shorten you, especially in a chubby jacket.

Italian company Moncler makes the most flattering puffy coats in all lengths—they frequently collaborate with top designers to customize their garments, so even though the jackets are expensive, you'll get a lot of flattering details incorporated into the design that ordinarily are impossible to find in run-of-the-mill parkas.

FUR: Every winter since the 1980s, fur has been a huge fashion trend. It's no surprise these days to flip open a celebrity glossy magazine and see piles of A-listers and clingers-on looking like they just raided the local zoo.

If you're going to buy into this trend, be careful. Arguments for animal welfare aside, fur is responsible for many fashion crimes—one wrong move and you could end up looking like a woolly mammoth.

Here's how to avoid looking like you just stepped off a fat farm in that new pelt.

DO opt for a short fur jacket with a narrow collar and capelet proportions. Combined with an upswept hairdo and a plunging neckline, this jacket will create a long, lean, and elegant silhouette.

DO use fur sparingly. An understated, simple top with fur details at your collar, hem, and at the end of your sleeves will draw attention to your slender wrists, elegant neck, and collarbone.

DO use fur as an accessory. Wearing a fur shrug is a great way to cover up your upper arms. A pared-down, simple design exudes femininity, and a carefully chosen collar will frame your face and make you—not the skins—the center of attention.

DO choose a body-skimming short-haired coat. The less bulk, the better, especially when choosing longer lengths. A light-colored coat with a dark outfit underneath will make you look slimmer—the dark against the light will make your body look like it's sunk farther into the coat. If you're wearing a dark coat, wear dark colors underneath as well.

DON'T go with oversized, long-haired, and blousy. You'll look like a Shar-Pei.

DON'T get too frilly. Even the best knockout body will go MIA underneath furry swirls, big lapels, and frou-frou.

DON'T swathe yourself in a fur blanket in public.

DON'T be a human snowball. Leave the Pomeranian look to the Pomeranians. If you pick a snowball coat, it will look like your coat ate your neck. Furthermore, don't button up high necklines. Period.

Chapter 10
ACCESSORIES

*W*hether or not we'd like to admit it, we all have silhouette-subversive items lurking in our closets. The truth is, even the most seasoned fashionista can fall victim to fattening accessories.

Sometimes crazy trends play saboteur—horizontally striped neon legwarmers, anyone?—and other times the allure of sparkly metallic ankle straps may become too much to resist. But don't panic—there are some simple rules we can apply to accessories regardless of season or ever-fleeting trend.

Here are my top tips on how to make your bling work for you.

Hats

Tip your hat: For centuries, painters have relied on the technique of *chiaroscuro,* Italian for "light and shadow," to define the human face on canvas. And, for almost as long, milliners have used the interplay of light and shadow to enhance the human face.

TILT THE FEDORA TO MATCH THE ANGLE OF YOUR JAWLINE.

Sadly, the popularity of the hat has been declining steadily since the 1950s, but the good news is that hats are back—and now there are dozens of great designers and hundreds of great styles to choose from.

Peering out from under a jauntily angled brim adds a touch of mystery and instant sophistication to even the most casual outfit. And what's more, strategic tilting emphasizes the delicate lines of your cheekbones and, when worn correctly, can simultaneously mirror and define your jawline.

STAY AWAY FROM: Skullcaps. You'll look like a tube of toothpaste with a tight skullcap on—everything from the ears down will look relatively huge in comparison. This is one of those trends that only models, with their spindly limbs, doe eyes, and elongated figures, can pull off. Do not attempt under any circumstances—

unless, of course, you're the civilian version of Naomi Campbell, who looks like a goddess in crystal-studded skullcaps. Are you Naomi Campbell?

GET: A fedora. Philip Treacy and Stephen Jones, two really important British milliners, make some of the sexiest and best-proportioned fedoras on earth. But you can find fedoras almost anywhere—your father's closet (perhaps a gift from his father), or at any decent hat shop or vintage store. I strongly recommend picking up a girl-fedora, as the men's versions tend to come in hokey colors and are a bit flat and mundane. Women's fedoras are more likely to be sexy and full of that too-cool-for-school attitude we should all work toward cultivating. Bonus: The brim protects you from harmful UV rays, thereby preventing wrinkles and making you look both thinner AND younger in the long run. Can't beat that with a stick!

Scarves

Chunky scarves are a model's best friend. True story told to me by a fashion designer at a very important fashion house: A super-famous model showed up the morning of a runway show so bloated and "fat" that the designer's ultra-skinny pants wouldn't button. What did the designer do (after panicking a LOT)? She loaded the model up with long, chunky scarves. No only can long scarves hide your belly paunch (and unbuttoned trousers), but, when repeatedly wound around your neck, they can also camouflage a double chin of nearly any magnitude.

STAY AWAY FROM: One single skinny, tie-width scarf wound tight around your neck. You might as well just tie a rope around your neck and declare yourself bound for the pigsty. The rule is: The proportions of your scarf should balance out your body proportions. Wispy models can wear ultra-skinny scarves because they're flat-chested and their arms are the width of my pinky.

GET SOME: Multicolored scarves and wear them all at once. If you're flat, they make you look bustier. If you're top-heavy, they distract from your boobiness. Wrap them up to your jawline to literally hide your double chin. The Gap makes some great patterns and lengths at prices so affordable you can buy a dozen. Okay, maybe not a dozen. How about three?

The Jackie hides jowls, a double chin, and your bedhead.

The Classic Flight Attendant

The classic flight attendant hides a saggy neck and double chin.

The Lacroix Scarf

The classic Lacroix is so chic and so French. Great over a simple sheath dress, it's a great proportion-balancing accessory when a necklace would be too spare. Excellent in situations where things go all pear-shaped.

The Simulated V-Neck

The simulated V-neck, for crewneck emergencies. Even if you're wearing the wrong neckline, you still can be a wannabe V-necker with a pretty scarf knotted just so. It draws attention to the center of your body. About 85 percent as effective as a real V neck.

HOW TO HIDE YOUR HOSTILE DOUBLE CHIN!

THE "FAMOUS"

SWEATER-AS-SCARF TRICK!

← IN SIX ILLUSTRATED STEPS…

The French-style sweater-as-scarf: Hands-down the most effective way to fake a perfect jawline, especially in photos.

To achieve the casual French "I just threw this around my neck and doesn't it look fabulous and look I'm all cheekbones and jawline" look, it's best to start with a fine-gauge black cashmere sweater, though cotton knits and lighter wools like merino will work too. Synthetic knits like viscose are too floppy.

Carefully fold it over itself from the sleeves down, flat-wrap it twice around your neck, and tuck in the ends. This is the most slimming "scarf" since it's not as wide or as twisted and bulky as a traditional scarf. Furthermore, the lines of a folded fine-gauge sweater are far more straight than the bulkiness of a knit scarf.

Final bonus: If it gets cold, you can actually put the sweater on your body.

This looks especially chic and très French topping a black sleeveless sheath dress. Super-slimming, my petite powder puff.

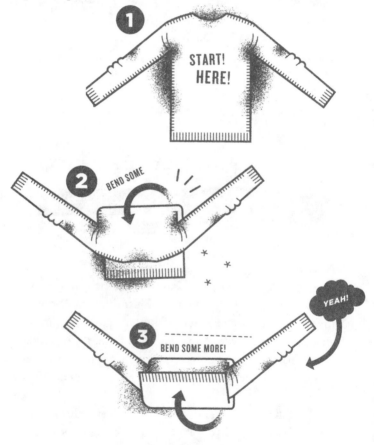

1

START!
HERE!

2 BEND SOME

3 BEND SOME MORE!

YEAH!

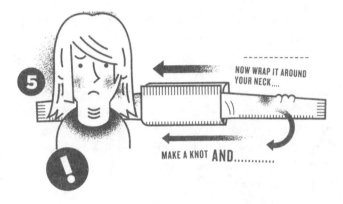

Hosiery

TIGHTS: As for tights, less is more: Unless you're a model, or just happen to have model-thin legs, patterned or colored tights will make your thighs and calves appear thicker than you'd like. Sorry, "tights-are-a-fashion-statement" people (you know who you are), it's a fact.

For a more chic and streamlined look, go barelegged (try spray-on stockings if you're scarred or marred), with sheer black, or with matte opaque black stockings (with an opacity gauge of 60+ denier).

STAY AWAY FROM: Argyle tights, large-hole fishnets, Fairisle-patterned tights. It's not that I don't recognize the woolly warm appeal of fresh-from-the-mists-of-Ireland patterned tights, but if your aim is to look lithe, avoid them. Sorry. You wouldn't wear big furry caterpillars on your legs (even if they were fabulous, fashionable, trendy caterpillars from the mists of Ireland), now, would you?

GET SOME: Old Navy's opaque tights are a total steal for under $5 (sometimes they even go on sale!). H&M (in selected cities) stocks a terrific 60-denier opacity long legging. And Donna Karan's sheer black hosiery is the sexiest, slickest splurge at about $17 a pop. Donna's tights? Make your legs look like they're shrouded in the most subtle, slimming, candlelight-esque shadow.

If you get to the U.K., take yourself to a Marks & Spencer (there's one on practically every block in London) for some of their bargain-priced 60-denier black tights. They're ultra-opaque and virtually indestructible. Seriously, some of mine have outlasted entire pairs of designer jeans.

For a bit of extra support, try Spanx brand control-top tights. They're a celeb favorite. Oprah claims she never goes a day without Spanx.

Socks

Shh! It's secret socks: If you absolutely must wear socks, keep it on the down low by donning secret socks— the socks that hide in your shoes. Socks that cut off your leg at the ankle or halfway up your calf make your legs look shorter and stumpy stumpy stumpy.

Gold Toe brand secret socks, available in multipacks at department stores everywhere, are the gold standard for athletic secret socks. They don't slide down and they last forever.

STAY AWAY FROM: Tube socks pulled up, mid-calf socks, trouser socks—the latter are not automatically, universally evil, but if you can see the tops of the trouser socks when you sit down, you're asking for trouble.

Gloves

Fat forearms? Think about gloves as boots for your arms. Just as wearing taller boots slims and lengthens the legs, long gloves have the same effect. Dark colors, natch, work the best. In the winter, your jacket covers up your arms, but in the autumn and spring, your arms are bare. Though it may seem odd at first, pair long, casual knit gloves, glovelets, or sleeves with a sleeveless top or plain sheath dress and you'll be the chicest talk of the town.

STAY AWAY FROM: Wrist-length chunky ski gloves or mittens—they shorten your arms by cutting them off at your wrist. This might seem like an obvious taboo, but in fact it is one of the most common mistakes women make. Instead, look for gloves that end at least halfway up your forearms—the closer to your elbow the better. If you're not comfortable with gloves this long, buy long knit ones and scrunch them down to a length you're comfortable with.

GET SOME: Long, knit gloves can be pulled up or scrunched down to taste. The most flattering length? Mid-upper arm. Make sure your gloves aren't too tight to pull this off—you don't want your upper arms to look like a couple of sausages.

Belts

Celebs love big belts, and that's not just because they look cool. In lieu of hip-hugging wide-waistband pants, the next best way to create the illusion of a tiny waist (and a smaller bum) is to sling a wide belt around your hips.

STAY AWAY FROM: Skinny belts cinched tight around your middle are a strict no-no. Especially if you plan on tucking your shirt in, which I don't recommend anyway. You'll just wind up looking squished and short-waisted.

GET SOME: Big studded belts. They're fantastic, sparkly, and fun. But they can be as pricey or even pricier than the pants they're meant to saddle. So check out discount retailers, especially online, and hit up your local vintage or secondhand store. They look a bit better worn in anyway.

Sunglasses

Fashion people love big sunglasses. Fashion editors looooooooove big sunglasses. Not only can they sit there, shrouded behind their super-dark shades, surreptitiously judging everyone around them, but the bigger the sunglasses, the smaller everything else on their faces looks. Huge squareish ones are by far the most flattering.

STAY AWAY FROM: Whatever you do, don't get John Lennon round sunglasses. Everything looks rounder when you put those on your face—your face, your nose, your nostrils. Ew.

GET SOME: Big squareish sunglasses in amber, dark brown, or black. The more monochromatic the better. Dior and Chanel, obviously, if you can afford it, but the $5 street vendor makes some pretty hot totty as well.

Handbags

> **"The bigger your bag is, the smaller you look carrying it. Almost like the body-friendly version of what Nicole Richie and Mary-Kate Olsen already know when it comes to making their faces look freakishly small with those gargantuan sunglasses."**
> **—Jenn Cohn, fashion publicist**

Many women don handbags like they pull on sweatpants—without a second thought. We've all witnessed the disastrous results—large ladies sporting tiny Vuitton backpacks are an all-too-common sight.

On the flipside, it's no mystery that the Hermès Birkin is the it-bag of the century. Besides the fact that it is absolutely gorgeous, the Birkin is one of the most flattering handbags on the market—toting its streamlined, structured body in the crook of your arm is nearly as slenderizing as a trick mirror.

Of course, you don't have to sell your right arm or your firstborn to get a bag that complements your figure. Here are some rules on how to pick yourself up a fabulous tote in any price range.

THE PERFECT BAG is a medium-structured tote (big enough to hold snacks) carried in the crook of your elbow. It draws attention to the forearm and wrist, which are, for most women, among the slimmest body parts. Bonus: If you eat too much, you can use your tote to cover up your tummy.

THE RULES

- DON'T carry a tiny bag unless you're tiny.
- DON'T carry a big floppy bag if you're big and floppy.
- DON'T wear a strap across your body. It makes you look fat from the front.
- DON'T wear a backpack. It makes you look fat from the side.

- DON'T wear a fanny pack. What is it, 1975, and are you roller-skating too?

> "Do not carry an over-size bottle of water around or a big bottle of fat-free ranch dressing in your purse. All the big girls in high school did this."
> —**William Van Meter, journalist**

TIPS

- It's all about balancing your proportions.
- If you're pear-shaped, shoulder your bag.
- If you're top-heavy, tote your tote.
- For the most modern look of all, leave your bag at home. This does not mean "stuff your pockets." It means: Take shorter trips.

SHOPPING CHEAT SHEET FOR THE THINGS PEOPLE BUG ME ABOUT MOST (BOTH FAT AND NON-FAT RELATED); REGARDLESS OF QUERY, ALL TIPS ARE SLIMMING

See Appendix for Where to Buy

BEST SCARVES FOR LAYERING: American Apparel's cotton scarves; Gap patterned scarves

BEST BRAS FOR BIG BOOBS: Freya; Fantasie; Wacoal

BEST CORSETS: Mr. Pearl; Agent Provocateur

BEST BODYSHAPER: Rago Shapewear; Hanes Maximum Control

BEST TOPS SIZED BY BRA SIZE: Bravissimo for sleeveless cotton tops and tanks

BEST CASUAL TOPS: American Apparel; Old Navy Perfect Fit tees; Splendid

BEST SUITS UP TO SIZE 20: Chanel

BEST PLACE TO BUY CHANEL: Reciproque Paris; Chanel Factory Stores

BEST SLIMMING TOP DESIGNER LABELS: Lanvin; Yves Saint Laurent

BEST SLIMMING BRIDGE LABELS: Tahari; BCBG; Club Monaco

BEST SLIMMING MALL LABELS: American Apparel; H&M; James Perse

BEST FANCY SWEATS: Juicy Couture

BEST JEANS: Blue Cult, Kasil, Salt Works

JEANS FOR SIZE 14+ LADIES: Seven7 at Lane Bryant

FANCY SHOES FOR WIDE FEET: Constança Basto; Sergio Rossi; Eley Kishimoto

BEST BOOTS FOR WIDER CALVES: Ann Demeulemeester; Marina Rinaldi; Cole Haan

BEST EVERYDAY SNEAKERS: Converse

Part Two
Shake It Up

I'm one of those people who, on fashion grounds alone, dislikes holidays and special occasions. Everyone thinks I'm just a little dark goth cloud, but in reality my main issue is that I have enough trouble dressing myself on a normal day-to-day basis—confronted with a special occasion, my closets just can't satisfactorily produce.

So it's with great pride that I present a section all about what you can do when your wardrobe is called upon to accommodate extraordinary circumstances—which, in my mind, includes everything from attending formal events, dressing up for Halloween, and going to the gym.

I learned a great deal while researching these chapters; here are the best *How Not to Look Fat* techniques I've found.

Chapter 11

SPECIAL OCCASIONS

*T*HERE'S A WEDDING AND YOU'RE A GUEST: Once upon a time I heard about a girl who wore a lace bustier dress to a friend's daytime wedding. Regardless of whether the bustier was slimming or not, this is wrong.

The number-one consideration for a wedding guest is to dress appropriately. A wedding day is the bride's day—it's her time to shine, not yours. This doesn't mean you have to look shlumpy, though. Wear something tasteful and tailored—try a simple sheath dress. So many people show up at nuptials in flowing floral skirts—let me be the first to say you shouldn't even own a flowing floral skirt.

Instead, your wardrobe ought to be chock-full of understated tailored dresses in flattering colors and subdued patterns. Understated? Subdued? Sure. Even if you're required to be dressier, it's easier to gussy up a blank palette like an elegant black or cream-colored dress than to tone down the botanical gardens.

THERE'S A WEDDING AND YOU'RE A BRIDE: For most brides-to-be, choosing the right gown is one of the most important parts of the planning process. With literally thousands of dresses to choose from, the task can be pretty daunting.

If you're walking down the aisle and plan to buy off the rack, you can take comfort in the fact that, for the most part, wedding dresses are incredibly flattering. Also, no matter what you choose to wear, you'll surely be beautiful on your wedding day—it will be one of the happiest days of your life.

The Structured Wedding Dress.

The structured boatneck sleeveless wedding dress is a classic that looks good on almost anyone. If you're concerned about your arms, choose a style with lace sleeves that act as coverups.

(That, and all the stress leading up to your wedding will surely take a toll on the appetite. I can't think of one bride I know who hasn't lost weight in the weeks leading up to the ceremony.)

That said, the key to finding the perfect dress is to consider your favorite features. Most women like their shoulders, and if you do, you should bare them. Iconic brides of years past have all had spectacular gowns that suited their personality and emphasized their best features.

Gracy Kelly, who is still known as a beacon of flawless taste, chose a modest wedding gown that showed off her slender, long neck and elegant arms.

Carolyn Bessette Kennedy's dress showed off her flawless collarbone and gorgeous shoulders.

Find your best parts—whether they be your back, your neck, or even your wrists, and pick a dress that exhibits them at their best.

Formals and Fancy Dress

For normal people like you and me, formal events come around once in a blue moon. I don't know about you, but as soon as I get a black-tie invitation, I have a debilitating bout of rapid-onset panic attack over finding something to wear. To be completely honest, 90 percent of the reason I skipped my senior prom in high school was because I couldn't figure out what I was going to wear. And dealing with my black-tie-gala-phobia certainly has not gotten easier over the years.

Top-heavy girls who don't mind baring some shoulder should opt for a halter-top dress with a drop-waist sash—the halter supports the chest while the sash creates a defined waistline.

While dressing to be a wedding guest is all about the bride, dressing for a formal occasion is likely going to be all about you—you and your problem spots.

See, there's very little leeway in the protocol for formal dressing. You don't have to worry about your legs because, oftentimes, the dress is long. But if your legs are your best feature, long dresses pose a problem.

The best way to tackle eveningwear is to examine your flaws—not your attributes. This is because since formal dressing is so limited, you'll have so little to work with in terms of variance in styles that you might as well just salvage what you can by making sure you cover up the things that make you cringe.

For example: If you dislike your arms, find a dress with sleeves. If you have back fat, avoid backless dresses. If you have a poochy tummy, choose a corseted dress or one with boning.

Sleeves for Chubby Arms.

Though hard to find, formal gowns with sleeves are out there! Check bridal stores or theknot.com for bridesmaid dresses—they tend to be more modest here than those in the generic prom section at your local department store.

Chapter 12
GYM CLOTHES

Like many of you, I hate working out—to me, going to the gym is exhausting, time-consuming, and boring. Never mind the fact that there's nothing grosser than public, communal sweating.

To top off the exercise experience—and as if to add insult to injury—workout clothes tend to be seriously unflattering.

Think about it—what are fat people supposed to wear to the gym? Baggy old T-shirts and shorts are too embarrassing (and uncomfortable) for words. But, on the other hand, if you ever saw me in a racer-back sports bra and bicycle shorts, I'd have to kill you.

This chapter is dedicated to those of you who are inspired to actually do something about your body—and to those of you who, like me, will wander accidentally into a gym twice a decade.

There's nothing more demoralizing than looking fat in the aerobics-class mirror. Here are five tips to make exercise as un-humiliating as possible.

(Just remember that as a last resort you can always wear sunglasses and hope no one recognizes you.)

TIP 1: Minimize the jiggle with a top that doubles as a sports bra—pick a solid-color top that has body-contouring panels around the tummy and bust line. Problems with bingo wings (you know, the flap of skin under the arm that jiggles when you shout "Bingo" and wave your winning card in the air)? Slip on a slim-fitting zip-up hoodie on top—unzip it halfway for a flattering V-shaped neckline.

TIP 2: Pick the right pants—choose a matte, stretchy, boot-cut pair of pants with a wide waistband to hide the rolls in your tummy. The fat-containing stretch combined with a proportion-balancing boot-cut will make you look longer and leaner. The most slenderizing inseam ends at your lower calf—high enough to show off your ankle-skinniness. If you have fat ankles, either wear leg warmers or longer pants.

TIP 3: Wrap it up—to look both sexy and slim at the gym, pick up one of the newly ubiquitous lightweight wrap gym tops. They're oh-so-soft, super-flattering on all shapes and sizes, and the adjustable draping is fat-concealing in places you need it most.

TIP 4: Wear secret socks—sneakers are so bulky, and if you wear fat socks on top, you'll look weighted down by your footwear. Avoid the chunk by always choosing secret socks—the ones that disappear into your shoes.

TIP 5: Lie down a lot—your spine elongates when you lie flat on the floor, making you look taller and longer, and your stomach seem flatter. In yoga class, they call it the corpse pose. Out on the floor, pass it off as stretching. Hidden bonuses to lying down: You'll sweat less and no one will be able to see your butt.

TOP TIP: If you're bouncing so much it's uncomfortable, put on another bra. There's no rule saying you're only allowed to wear one. Wearing your regular bra underneath a sports bra not only provides terrific support, preventing damage to breast tissue, but it also prevents the dreaded uni-boob by lifting and separating and not just squishing.

Chapter 13
SWIMWEAR

Swimsuits are, possibly, the one item that women hate shopping for more than jeans. Whereas jeans can cover and contain the jiggle, swimsuits let it all hang out there.

While I can't promise you you'll hit the beach looking like a Baywatch babe, I can talk you through the best swimwear styles and help you find something that might work for you.

EXPERT TIP: "The less clothes you wear the thinner you look. This especially works on the beach—a skimpy string bikini is way more flattering than boy shorts and a bra top—or in bed—skimpy undies scream supermodel skinny but a floor length nightie cries out wobbly old grandma."

—Sarah Tomczak, author of *How to Be a Sex Goddess*

The modestly sexy HALTER TOP BIKINI provides great support for up to a DD cup—any larger than that and you might strain your neck. Look for a wide band at the rib cage to provide more support. The extra band of

fabric makes the bikini seem less skimpy against a large bosom, and the halter draws the eye to the neck, minimizing a broader, bulkier torso.

Everyone wants to wear TRIANGLE BIKINIS, just like the Hawaiian Tropic Girls. If you are above a B cup, I implore you to choose an underwired triangle top (from swimwear labels like Venus Swimwear and Milla) that provides lift and support for the twins. Ever watch televised spring breaks and see big boobs bursting out from under non-underwire triangle tops? Some grody men think this is hot. The rest of the worst thinks it looks sloppy. And sloppy = fat.

Standard UNDERWIRE BIKINI TOPS should be a part of every woman's summer wardrobe, especially if you have narrow shoulders and big boobs. It's all about the support—and choosing a non-halter can balance out a narrow frame.

When purchasing a TANKINI follow the same guidelines as when selecting a top. V-necks are more flattering and a longer top prevents lumping, especially when you sit. Stay away from horizontal patterns and stripes.

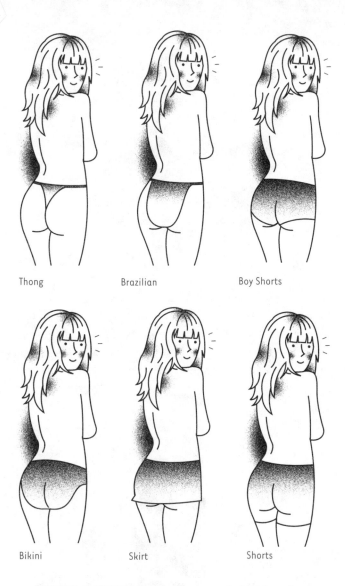

Thong

Brazilian

Boy Shorts

Bikini

Skirt

Shorts

BIKINI BOTTOMS are a personal decision, but my personal recommendation is to pick the Brazilian bottom with a tie side. The cut of the Brazilian somehow makes

HOW NOT TO LOOK FAT

your butt look like it only takes up that much space, and the ties allow you to adjust the tightness of the sides so they don't cut into your hip fat and cause lumping.

If you have your heart set on a patterned swimsuit, choose a pattern that's centered around the middle of your body. Chevron stripes and circles are particularly flattering.

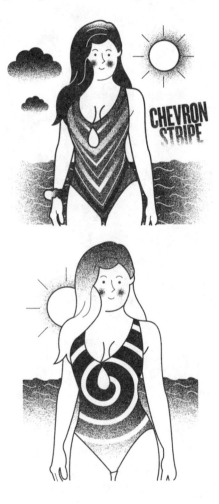

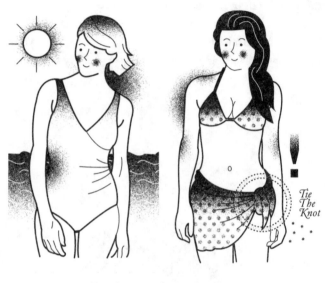

Wrap One-Piece   Sarong

THE WRAP ONE-PIECE has the same magic that's in a wrap dress—it instantly creates a waist where once there was just pooch. L.L. Bean makes some great figure-fixing ones.

Don't just throw a SARONG over yourself; if you don't tie it right, you'll just look like you're swathed in a blanket. Angle the sarong downward—start at the top of one hip and tie it at the bottom on the other hip. Again, drawing the eye downward emphasizes the waist and the womanly curvature of your hips.

When choosing a COVER UP, go simple. Avoid pockets, buttons, embroidery, or gimmicks. A simple scoop-

H.O.T.

SHOWS THE TOP OF YOUR THIGH!

neck chemise-length tank dress is the best. Pick a body-skimming one that has side vents and watch heads turn as you casually stroll down the beach.

NO-FAIL SOLUTION: If all else fails, buy a professional tank suit—like a Speedo—in black. Don't worry about the high neck and low-cut leg. Seals aren't thin, but when they're wearing shiny black from head to toe, don't they look sleek?

TOP TIP: When lying on your beach towel, extend your arms straight over your head for a flatter-looking tummy. Probably not the most comfortable position, but slimming!

Swimwear

Chapter 14

FEASTS

*T*here's nothing harder than getting dressed for a big family meal. Besides the basic trauma of trying to find clothes roomy enough to accommodate your post-meal tummy, there's the anxiety of your outfit being subject to the critical scrutiny of family and close friends.

So—purely for research purposes, of course—I decided to stuff myself silly on a large dinner to see if it's possible to avoid looking like a big turkey butterball after dinner.

The conclusion? Even though they say you are what you eat, I say you can have your fat and eat it too—and still look great!

Here are my favorite tips on how to look cute, be comfortable, win your mother's approval, and manage to eat a lot all at once.

PROBLEM: Post-meal tummy distend.

Solution 1: Stay seated for as long as possible.

The easiest way to hide your turkey baby is to stay put. Sit up straight so that the only parts that show are from the bust upward. Cover your pooch with a napkin and mumble something about your high heels being uncomfortable to stand in. They don't call it sitting pretty for nothing!

Solution 2: Scarves

Sneaky!

YOUR
FANCY
SHAWL...

HIDES YOUR
OPEN BUTTON!

Remember what models do when they can't button their pants before a fashion show? They layer up with long scarves to hide their tummies (and the offending undone button). Pull a "fat man on the couch"—unbutton your trousers after dinner and cover up your stealthy secret with loads of distracting, colorful scarves. Remember that looking top-heavy minimizes everything from the waist down—so don't be afraid to sport more than one!

PROBLEM: Pants too tight.
Solution: Invest in Lycra.

Conventional wisdom should dictate that everyone be allowed to wear sweatpants to Thanksgiving dinner. Unfortunately, conventional wisdom doesn't have a clue about fashion, so go for the second-best option by investing in clothes made with Lycra. Pick leg-lengthening two percent Lycra boot-cut jeans (most denim brands make at least one pair) with a super-low rise that won't oppress that second helping of pecan pie.

PROBLEM: Shirt too tight.
Solution 1: Wear a loose, tailored button-down.

Everyone knows that the most flattering clothes are tailored pieces, but how do you wear tailoring to a family dinner without looking like you dressed for the office? Find your solution at any of your local shirtmakers, which are sure to be stocked with fun and flirty pastel tailored shirts that feature slimming vertical patterns like herringbone and tuxedolike details. Turn up the collar to frame your face and to create the illusion of an elongated neck. Dress up your shirt with a pretty scarf and colorful cufflinks.

Solution 2: Carry a cardigan.

So you showed up to dinner in a slinky, body-skimming top and now you're so fat you're too embarrassed to get up? Avoid this situation entirely by toting a pretty cardigan along with you—skip the shawl and wrap, they're too fussy and dressy for indoor meals. Pick a V-neck three-quarter-sleeve cardi that's decorated with festive beads. Button accordingly—leave it open at the top and secure it around your waist for a slimming, hourglass silhouette.

Solution 3: Sparkle at the extremes.

Draw attention to your wrists and neckline by choosing a flattering V-neck shirt that has sequins and beading around the cuffs and neckline. The details will make your arms look longer and draw attention to your skinny collarbone area.

Chapter 15

COSTUMES

*B*lubber bubble toil and trouble is right.

When Halloween rolls around and your posterior (or whatever problem areas you might have—mine is the area between my jaw and my ankles) just isn't agreeing with your old standby costumes anymore, what's a girl to do?

You either can throw up your hands and go to Halloween parties dressed as nothing this year (lame, rude, lazy) or you can buck up and get yourself a sexy, figure-flattering new look.

There are a few simple rules for finding a great-looking getup—like, don't dress up as a barnyard animal—but don't expect to score a killer outfit at your local five-and-dime.

Your best bet? Head to a reputable costume shop, where you'll have hundreds of choices, expert advice, and access to fitting rooms where you can try before you buy (or rent).

Read on to get the skinny on how to hide your fat festively this holiday weekend.

Rules

1. Get a costume that fits: Choose body-skimming looks like period costumes and almost-contemporary real clothes. Jumpsuits are flattering if they're made of thick stretch fabrics and aren't skintight head to toe. Way-oversized getups will make you look short and dumpy, and too-tight ensembles probably will get you arrested by the sausage patrol. Translation: Just say no to catsuits and plush pumpkin sacks.

Jumpsuits are very flattering. A huge stand-up collar elongates the neck, and a chunky, drop-waist belt elongates the torso.

2. Show slim skin: This rule is elementary—if it's flabby, cover it up! Don't go sleeveless if you're afflicted with bingo wings, and skip the miniskirts if you're worried about cellulite. Instead, flaunt your skinniest features

The French Maid!

Even though it may look skimpy, the French Maid costume covers the upper arms and butt. Adding an apron can cover up a tummy pooch. Plus, you can wear black stockings.

foolproof body parts on most people include collarbones and wrists. Whatever you do, don't be a beer-belly dancer.

3. Androgyny will always be hot. And tailoring shaves off pounds. If you're looking for a bit of shape and structure, don a zoot suit or sharp pinstripes and be an old-school gangster moll. Don't forget the fedora! Wear it with attitude to match and guys will fall at your feet.

4. Get a costume with a waist. Better yet, a corset. If, like me, you'll be covering up as much as you can, pick an outfit that has a defined, waist-narrowing silhouette. Corsets—

inside or outside—automatically give you an hourglass figure, no matter what you're wearing. Think "wench."

5. Accessorize wisely: Got a chubby face? A great wig will not only hide your facial flab, but also can give you instant cheekbones and an air of mystery—Who is that fabulous girl anyway? A sexy hat worn at a jaunty angle will draw attention to your jawline and lips. And a flirty prop—think feather duster or, um, whip—distracts the eye. Concentrate on drawing attention toward your extremities—feet, hands, top of head—for a body-lengthening effect.

Gangster Girl ®

Part Three
Primpin' Ain't Easy

If you've ever picked up a copy of *Star, Us Weekly,* or *In Touch* magazine, you'll have had a close encounter with the third kind—otherwise known as the celebrity *sans* makeup and hair-styling.

It's true—when they're not intentionally vamping for the camera, most celebs wander the streets of Los Angeles and New York looking like upside-down brooms with faces.

It just goes to show that no matter how skinny you may be, poor grooming can leave you looking sloppy, shiny, frazzled, and bloated—and none of these things make you feel thinner or better about yourself.

Besides, what's the point of putting all that effort into selecting what to put on your body if you don't take care of the body itself? From hair-styles to makeup tricks to fancy spa treatments, here is how to maximize your skin-deep svelte potential.

Chapter 16
HAIR

*I*f you knew that something was unflattering, would you wear it every day?

Probably not—so why do so many women wear bad hairstyles day in and day out all year-round? You've only got one face, and your hair is its best and most powerful accessory. Whether your mug is round, oval, heart-shaped, or square—a little snip-snip here and a snip-snip there can make all the difference in how people perceive your facial girth.

While super-long, blunt-cut hair is great on towering, waiflike models, the same style can make an average girl look shorter and squatter. On the other hand, soft, face-framing layers can do wonders for camouflaging chubby cheeks and jowls—it's no wonder the "Rachel" haircut was such a hit in the '90s.

The right hairstyle can also do wonders for your physical proportions. For example, if you're pear shaped, avoid slicked-back dos unless you're keen on the pinhead look. On the other hand, if you're top-heavy, don't pull a big-headed tease—you'll look like you're about to topple over.

So what's the best hairstyle?

"It all depends on the shape of the face and your lifestyle," says celebrity hairstylist Frederic Fekkai. "As a rule of thumb, growing bangs out and cutting simple layers tends to elongate the face and give the illusion of a thinner face. And keep hair shiny and sleek, not poofy and dull!"

Face-Slimmin'
RACHEL'S NINETIES FAME QUIFF!

HAIRCUT HALL OF FAME: THE RACHEL:

"Every woman needs to have some softness around her face," says stylist Shin of Paul Labrecque Salon & Spa on Manhattan's Upper East Side. "When your hair just sits on your head, people can see the full perimeter of your face."

EXPERT TIP: "Use shampoo that builds body—flat hair on bigger faces makes the face look bigger."
—Liz Sullivan, fashion photographer

HAIRCUT HALL OF FAME: THE HEIDI:
Face-framing long layers and chunky bangs severely limit
what you're allowed to see. If Heidi had any fat on her
face (she doesn't, I've checked), we wouldn't be able to
see it anyway.

Hair

HAIRCUT HALL OF FAME: THE FABULOUS ITALIAN MOVIE STAR: Sideswept bangs are just amazing. The fringe length depends on how big your forehead is—and it's an inverse relationship. If you have a smallish forehead, get longer sideswept layered bangs so that the longest pieces just reach behind your ears. If you have a bigger forehead, get shorter ones. Sorry, no bang-tucking for you.

HAIRCUT HALL OF FAME: THE PENÉLOPE:
If you're short, like under 5′4″, and not model-skinny, don't grow your hair longer than two inches below your shoulder. Hair any longer will make you look shorter and fatter.

Generally, you'll look taller and slimmer with hair between shoulder and jaw length. It's brave to go shorter—if you're chubby, it's just not a good idea. If you're skinny, everyone will call you pixieish.

Of course, there's also the bald look to consider. Bald is hot. But you have to have a gorgeous, slim, angular face with high cheekbones to pull that one off.

Hair

Chapter 17
MAKEUP

*W*hen it comes right down to it, body fat is pretty easy to hide. While muumuus won't make you look any thinner, they easily can serve as last-ditch shrouds for any rolls of blubber you may harbor.

Unfortunately, sack dresses end at the neck. The harsh reality is that it's pretty hard to get away with fat on the face. What are you going to do? Put on a mask? Start wearing a burka?

A more practical (and less factional) option can be found in the cosmetics aisle at your local drugstore. Using different shades of foundation, blush, eye shadow, and bronzer, you can make your double chin, chubby cheeks, and puffy eyes practically disappear!

You don't even need to splash out on expensive department store makeup to get quality and expert advice on how to slim your facial features.

I enlisted the help of Melissa Silver, a celebrity makeup artist, whose clients include Renée Zellweger (thin!), Heidi Klum (thin!), and Cindy Crawford (thin!), to show us effective, natural-looking facial contouring techniques using only products by super-affordable Maybelline New York.

Her best tips? Pick mocha brown colors that have a slightly pearly sheen—duller gray-browns can end up looking like dirt. And super-frosty colors, which are harder to blend, might leave you looking like what shall from here on in be called Big Sick Baby—shiny, a little sweaty, and bloated.

It's super-important to practice at home before debuting your "skinny" face in public. Experiment in natural light (read: by a window), and apply a little bit of color at a time. Step back from the mirror every few strokes to evaluate the results.

Remember: It's easier to add more makeup later than to take excess away.

Read on for more tips on how to slenderize and structure five key features on your magnificent mug.

EYES: Too much shimmer can make your eyelids look puffy, especially in pictures. Instead of frosted shadow, look for iridescent pearl colors. Pre-coordinated color packs—like the neutral Maybelline Chocolate Mousse trio—make matching and blending a no-brainer.

NOSE: Give yourself an instant nose job by running a medium-size makeup brush dipped in mocha powder down the sides of your nose. Make sure to blend the color well—you don't want to walk around with dark vertical stripes running down the middle of your face. Also try dabbing a bit of the color on the inside corners of your eyes to narrow the bridge of your nose.

FOREHEAD: You can either get bangs or you can counter a well-endowed forehead by brushing contouring powder on your temples and along your hairline. Remember to blend or you might wind up looking like you just didn't wash your hair. Those with smaller foreheads should avoid this technique entirely.

CHEEKS: Using a medium to large brush, apply a warm brown-toned blush—like Maybelline's Mocha Velvet or Sierra Sand—in a sweeping motion (think: Nike swoosh) under and around the apples of your cheeks. Apply a warm coral or pink hue on the apples of your cheeks. Blend the whole thing upward and outward. *Voilà!* Instant cheekbones!

Quick fix: If you've put on too much color and don't have time to wash your face and start all over again, dust a little pressed powder over your cheeks to soften the look.

JAWLINE: To hide that double chin and neck jiggle, choose a contouring color that is about two shades darker than your natural skin tone. Brush it all along your jaw line in downward strokes beginning just under your earlobes and ending near where the corner of your mouth begins. Blend with a large brush and pressed powder.

FOOLPROOF TRICK: Minimizing shine with blotting papers or pressed powder instantly will make you look less sweaty, shiny, and bloated.

Chapter 18

HOW TO
SMELL THINNER

*I*f instantly appearing twelve pounds thinner with a simple sweat-free spritz of the perfume atomizer sounds too good to be true, you haven't yet met Dr. Alan Hirsch, the director of Chicago's Smell and Taste Treatment and Research Foundation.

In a study conducted over the course of a decade, Dr. Hirsch, the author of over one hundred articles on the psychological power of scent, found one scent combination that caused men to perceive women to be twelve pounds lighter.

"We didn't actually reduce the weight of women who wore the aroma, but, rather, caused men to believe she weighed less," said Dr. Hirsch. "[This scent] acts as the olfactory equivalent to vertical lines."

Originally conceived in an effort to find scents to improve the self-image of those with body dysmorphic disorder—like many anorexics who perceive themselves to be much larger than they really are—the experiment instead yielded a fragrance that altered men's perception of women's sizes. Dr. Hirsch could not find any odor that influenced a woman's perception of weight.

"Either women are too adroit at guessing other people's weight," suggests Dr. Hirsch, "or men are just easily influenced by how a woman smells."

The fragrance, a blend custom-made for the study by Charles Stebbens, president of Scientific Scents (makers of perfumes, fragrances, and flavors for consumer products like protein drinks and candles), features three notes, or layers, of scent.

The top note is spicy cinnamon—a fragrance that has been shown to increase the precision of motor skills and enhance an individual's ability to perform fine tasks. The base note is musk, a heavier scent used to prolong the lifespan and impact of the fragrance when worn.

The heart of the fragrance is a mixed floral that features rose, gardenia, lily of the valley, and hyacinth.

The rose—a climbing tea rose—acts as an enabler, Stebbens explains, allowing your olfactory passageways to become more receptive to sensitive smells. Hyacinth is excitatory—and also, generally, a well-liked scent. Gardenia acts as an intensifier, making the other scents surrounding it appear stronger.

Stebbens hypothesizes that it's the lily of the valley that has the most important effect in this fragrance. In chemoreception research, when positron emission tomography (PET), aka brain-wave scans, is performed on subjects who have been exposed to lily of the valley, responses are triggered in parts of the brain that correlate to size perception. Empirical tests have shown that those under the influence of lily of the valley tend to perceive themselves as larger in relation to objects around them.

Since this particular combination of six scents is not commercially available, you're best off mixing up your own batch. Use equal proportions of each scent and stick to natural perfume oils, staying away from synthetic scents, which may or may not have the same effect.

Sure, it's expensive to mix up even one batch, but how much would you be paying a trainer or a liposuctionist to rid you of those twelve pounds??

Chapter 19

SPA TREATMENTS

"Self-Tanner. Everywhere. Always."

—Emily Listfield, editor in chief of *Fitness* magazine

*W*ith swimsuit season just around the corner (who cares what time of year it is, swimsuit season is always too perilously close on my calendar), everyone is scrambling for the latest way to lose weight fast.

While exercise and dieting may provide long-term results, those who want immediate results are turning to spas and at-home beauty treatments for instant gratification.

Women spend almost $9 billion on spa treatments every year, and the global skincare market revenues top $31 billion every year.

Slimming and weight loss constitute one of the fastest-growing segments of the beauty industry, analysts say. Scientists are aggressively developing new techniques and ingredients for both professional and at-home use.

Intent on slimming down without setting foot in the gym, I set off to four of New York's most popular day spas to test out their newest fat-busting treatments.

While none of the treatments I tried last forever, they're great quick fixes right before special occasions or at times when you need a little ego boost—and with pampering spas springing up all over the country, you probably can find the same treatments near your home town.

ELECTRO MUSCLE STIMULATION "The scientific principle of this treatment is to induce muscle stimulation similar to exercise," explains Dr. Adrienne Denese of New York City's SkinScience Medical Spa, who I always see on public television giving seminars on skin care. She wires my stomach and thighs to a high-tech-looking machine. "This 45-minute treatment is the equivalent of simultaneously doing 450 crunches and 450 leg and butt lifts," she says.

The sensation of having my abs, butt, thighs, and hip muscles simultaneously contracted wasn't nearly as unpleasant as I had expected—it felt as if I were having a vibrating deep-tissue massage.

The results were remarkable. After one forty-five-minute session, I lost two inches from my waist and lower abdomen—a loss Denese said was permanent, thanks to a gain in muscle.

Four days later, my muscles were still tight.

(Then I ate pizza every day for two weeks straight.)

It isn't cheap, but it's like paying for two personal training sessions—minus the pain, the sweat, and the trainer—and with incredible results.

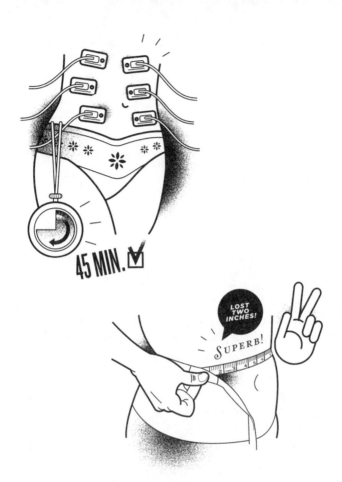

HIGH-VOLUME SCULPTED TAN "Air brush is so last year," says tanner-to-the-stars Sally Blenkey-Tchasova, the owner of New York City's Brazil Bronze.

Her spray-tan technique is turbine-powered, which means the pigment particles come out ultra-small and the application is ultra-smooth.

The high-volume tan took just three minutes to apply—and there were no bad-smelling fumes.

After giving me a base tan, Blenkey-Tchasova contoured me head to toe—including the sides of my stomach and my rear view—with a darker shade of tan. Even your face can be slimmed this way!

Instantly I had a defined tummy, high cheekbones, and a lifted toosh. My double chin disappeared and my hips looked (almost) Baywatch-worthy.

The tan lasts up to a week, so it's a perfect cost-effective treatment to get right before a special event.

ELECTRO-STIMULATION FACELIFT Want to get rid of that pesky gobble-gobble under your chin?

At New York Ciy's Completely Bare, specially trained spa technicians applied techno wands to the muscles in my face. An electrical current was passed between the wands, causing my facial muscles to contract and tighten.

Though it felt as if someone were pricking me over and over again with tiny needles for an hour, my jawline was visibly tightened and my cheekbones were more sharply defined afterward.

While the difference wasn't dramatic, friends told me my skin seemed to glow.

"The results last between forty-eight and seventy-two hours," says Cindy Barshop, owner of Completely Bare. "It's particularly effective on people with wrinkles or sagging skin, especially in the eye area."

ENDERMOLOGIE AND LYMPHATIC DRAINAGE For this treatment I tried the Cellulite Buster at New York City's Anushka Day Spa & Cellulite Clinic. As I lay on my stomach, anti-cellulite aesthetician Natasha vacuum-massaged my back, butt, and thighs with a roller similar to the one used in Endermologie treatments.

"The difference is that we incorporate ultrasound, which helps to stimulate circulation and melt the fat that causes cellulite," she explains.

After the massage, she zipped me into the Presso Jet, a large, blue plastic body sleeve that rhythmically inflated and deflated, massaging me from waist to ankle. This is supposed to stimulate lymphatic drainage of toxins and water weight.

The firm, pulsating massage action felt wonderful. And while I didn't have to visit the bathroom constantly afterward, as I had been warned I would, I did feel much thirstier than usual.

For the next two days, the cellulite on my butt and thighs was less visible and my skin was firmer and more toned.

Part Four
Walking the Walk

In *My Fair Lady,* one of my favorite films of all time, we learn that you can take the girl out of Soho, but you can't take the Soho out of the girl. Remember when Eliza, dressed as a perfect lady, attends Ascot for the first time? Despite Henry Higgins's best efforts, her potty mouth practically ruins the illusion they've both worked so hard to construct.

On the path to How Not to Look Fat enlightenment, there are innumerable saboteurs to which you may fall prey. While it's easy enough to dab on a bit of perfume or strap on a pair of sexy slingbacks, something as simple as a bad night's sleep, a bit too much salt, or standing with your toes pointed outward can destroy all your efforts.

This section is the icing on the cake—the "Faking It" part of the book that will make all the subtle difference in the world.

Chapter 20

SLEEP YOURSELF
THINNER

*I*f you thought sleep was a waste of time, I highly recommend active sleeping—utilizing your forty winks
to the best of their *How Not to Look Fat* potential.

Stack those pillows high—and do it in a tier formation. That way, you'll have graduated support for your shoulders and neck. Just think of this as utilizing gravity—as you sleep, gravity will draw the excess water away from your face, eyes, and head. You'll wake up far less bloated and with eyes far less puffy than you would ordinarily.

Each morning, when you wake up, before you put on your makeup (don't say a little prayer for me), take stock of both your upper and lower eyelids. If they are puffy, it's important to bring them down before applying eyeshadow. Otherwise you'll look puffy and tired all day. Besides the usual damp teabags, cold spoons, and bags of frozen peas the old wives tell tales about, I'd like to throw in my two cents and say that there are a ton of great eye treatments on the market today. MAC's Fast Response Eye Cream visibly tightens the undereye area within minutes. And DuWop's Eye Therapy masks are herbal treatments that help not only with bloating but with irritation and redness as well—they're reusable too!

Five Things to Do Before You Hit the Hay If You Want to Look Thinner in the Morning

1. Don't eat salt for six hours before you go to bed. Too much salt will make you retain water and none of your rings will fit the next morning.
2. Don't cry. Your whole face will puff up.
3. Make sure you have at least eight hours ahead of you. A rested body is a lean body.

4. Only eat lean protein, like tuna and egg whites, at dinner—protein doesn't cause you to retain water, as do products made with white flour.

5. Take off your makeup—sleeping in a faceful of the day's dirt and makeup can irritate your skin and eye area. Not only can this cause zits and redness, it can also cause your skin and eyes to puff up.

EXPERT TIP: "Take a boar-bristle hairbrush to your arms and legs. Brushing the skin on your upper arms and thighs will break down that cottage cheese (aka cellulite). A few weeks of brushing and you'll look skinnier than ever."

—Rebecca Beeson, fashion designer who dresses skinny stars like Paris Hilton, Lindsay Lohan, and Tori Spelling

Chapter 21

AVOID THE BLOAT

EXPERT TIP: "My number one piece of advice is this: Wear wide shoes and get a fat boyfriend. Everything is relative."

—**Stephanie Lessing, author of** *She's Got Issues*

IF YOU EAT THIS: Salt, Pasta, or Bread, you'll probably bloat. White flour and sodium-heavy foods are naturally water retentive, so don't be surprised if an hour after your meal your tummy sticks out and you're feeling a bit poofy.

TOP TIP: Nicholas Perricone, M.D., author of *The Perricone Weight-loss Diet*, recommends using a lot of spices in your food—particularly cinnamon, turmeric, or cloves. Spices are great fat burners; they help maintain blood sugar levels, and reduce cravings.

GET RID OF YOUR BLOAT WITH THESE:

Caffeinated cola, coffee, water. Flush out that extra water weight by drinking more water (I know, I know, counter-intuitive, but it works, okay?) and drinking moderate amounts of caffeinated products, which act as a mild diuretic. You'll be able to, literally, pee out some of that bloat.

Chapter 22

DRINKING

*N*ew York's most fashionable watering holes cater to celebrities, models, and all the city's other weight-obsessed denizens every night of the week.

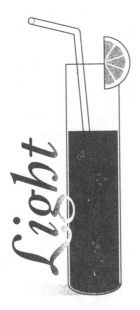

Serving rounds of newfangled, calorie-conscious drinks, bars are inspiring the smart set to forsake their beloved cosmos (so '90s!) in favor of skinny, lower-calorie mojitos and watermelon vodkas.

"There has been such a surge in diet and low-cal requests," says Jonathan Cheban, who handles the celebrity-packed hotspot AER Club & Lounge. "Diet Coke and Bacardi is one of our most popular drinks—especially with the models. We never even carried Diet Coke before."

Weight watchers have long struggled with the knowledge that downing trendy cocktails makes as much sense as burgling your own home.

"A traditional piña colada made with coconut milk can pack in more than 500 calories and 8 grams of fat per glass," says Cindy Sherwin, fitness director and nutritionist at The Gym on New York's Madison Square Park, "and popular fruit drinks like the cosmopolitan can measure 500 calories as well."

Since consuming 3,500 extra calories leads to a pound of weight gain, knocking back one drink a night for a full week can be a hazard to your weight-loss efforts.

That's why these days, instead of high-calorie cranberry and orange juice, people are going out of their way to request watermelon juice with their bottle service, says Cheban.

While watermelon vodkas are delicious, there also are options for those who crave the flavor of their old favorites.

Sydney Foster, dietician and personal trainer at the Sports Club/LA, suggests opting for hard liquor with a splash of fruit juice instead of an elaborate mixed drink. Grapefruit and watermelon are the two lowest-calorie juices typically found in bars.

The Sports Club/LA bar serves simple, light drinks alongside the usual suspects—vodka seltzer is a popular 80-calorie choice. And there are skinny mojitos, made with lime juice and less sugar.

For dedicated wine drinkers, there's the White Lie Early Season Chardonnay, which boasts 97 calories per 5-ounce glass (compared with the usual 129). Developed by female execs and vintners, it describes itself as "by women for women."

So whether you're an at-home mixologist or a dedicated barhopper, here's a sampling of my favorite skinny cocktails from around New York City. Bikini boot camp never tasted so good.

Rum Reduction

DON'T DRINK: Mojito (200 calories)
DRINK: Light Mojito, from The Sports Club/LA (130 calories)

2 tablespoons lime juice
3 mint sprigs, plus some leaves for garnish
Ice cubes
1 tablespoon sugar
Club soda
1.5 ounces light rum

Combine the lime juice and mint sprigs in a glass and muddle them together with a spoon. Add some ice, followed by the sugar and club soda. Pour the rum in last. Then garnish with mint leaves.

La Piña de Nada

DON'T DRINK: Piña colada (500 calories and up to 8 grams of fat from coconut milk)
DRINK: The Skina Piña (about 100 calories and 0 grams of fat)

1.5 oz. Malibu coconut rum
1.5 oz. sugar-free lemonade
1 oz. pineapple juice

Pour ingredients over ice and stir. Garnish with pineapple chunks or cocktail umbrella.

Dieter's Daiquiri

DON'T DRINK: Cherry rum daiquiri (400 calories)
DRINK: Dieter's daiquiri (about 100 calories and 0 grams of fat)

1.5 oz. berry-flavored rum—try Bacardi raspberry-flavored rum
Muddled black cherries
Club soda

Mix ingredients together. Garnish with a wedge of lime.

Barely Brazilian

DON'T DRINK: Berry Caipirinha (300 calories)
DRINK: Splendid Berry Caipirinha from New York's
Meatpacking District hotspot Lotus (190 calories)

4 chopped strawberries
2 tablespoons Splenda granular
Splash of sour mix
Splash of fresh strawberry puree
Ice cubes
1.7 ounces cachaca (Brazilian liquor)
1 lime slice, for garnish

Muddle together the strawberries, Splenda, sour mix,
and strawberry puree in a rocks glass. Add some ice and the
cachaca. Pour into a shaker and shake vigorously. Then pour
back into the rocks glass and garnish with a lime slice.

Chapter 23

EXERCISE?
IF YOU MUST

*T*here's nothing grosser than communal sweating, but some exercise is just SO worth it.

At my first Yoga class ever, my instructor told me that within her first year of practicing she had grown half an inch. I was sold. Listen, I'm 5'6" and all about aspirational puberty.

What's so gratifying about yoga is that you can feel the difference right away—as soon as you walk out of that studio your posture is better, you're taller, your muscles are tighter, and you're more clear headed. And, most important, your tummy is narrower—yoga is, after all, a core-conditioning practice.

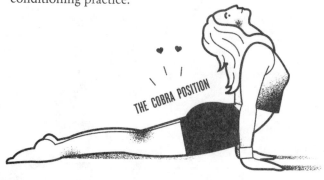

THE COBRA POSITION

THE DOWNWARD-FACING DOG POSITION

Pilates, allegedly practiced by sinewy stars like Sarah Jessica Parker, is similar in principle—it trains and conditions your core muscles so you stand up straighter and become leaner and longer (instead of bulky and squat).

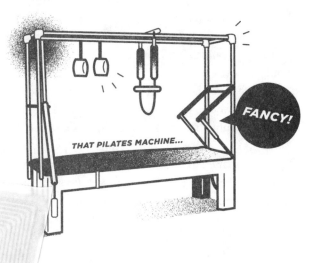

THAT PILATES MACHINE...

FANCY!

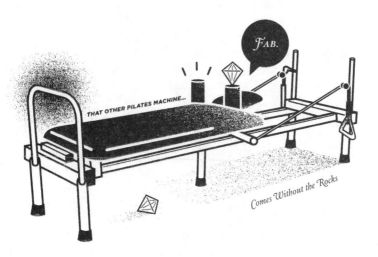

THAT OTHER PILATES MACHINE...

*F*AB.

Comes *Without the* Rocks

While one-on-one pilates training is pricey and time-consuming, most gyms now offer mat-based pilates classes, which don't require a whole lot of fancy equipment.

Still, yoga and pilates are long-term endeavors. What about quick fixes?

In my haze of laze, I bought an inversion machine off the Home Shopping Network last year. I call it the Batman machine because it hangs me upside down by my ankles—like the way I imagine Batman sleeps.

The sad thing is that when I made this purchase I thought I'd become a dedicated hanger—eventually working up to doing upside-down crunches and pull-ups. Whatever. The reality is that I'm too lazy to even strap myself into this thing and hang there, so now my inver-

5540

sion machine just sits in my living room and I manage to clamber into it about once every two months.

However, on the rare occasions when I do play Batman, I can feel and hear gravity working its magic on my spine—click-click-click and all my vertebrae are lined up again. That, and my stomach is instantly flatter because my back is straight. It's no-sweat genius for people who can't do headstands!

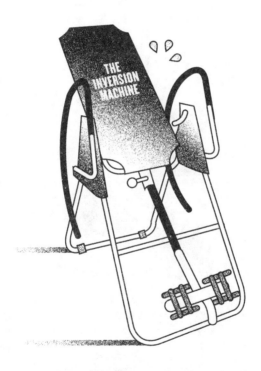

I got mine off the Home Shopping Network, and am so lazy I hardly ever use it, but when I do, it helps align my spine and stretch out my back muscles. Just think—all day long, gravity is pulling us down. Being stretched upwards, even if just for a minute a day, makes me walk taller and far more aware of my posture.

Headstand Exercise

In yoga, inversions, like headstands, help elongate the spine—some practitioners claim to grow up to half an inch in their first year! And you know what taller means: thinner-looking.

HOW NOT TO LOOK FAT

THE PLANK MOVE

BEST EMERGENCY FAT MOVE: The Plank. Prop yourself flat on your elbows and toes for one minute. Your tummy will be instantly tighter and flatter.

Chapter 24

THE CAMERA SUBTRACTS FIVE POUNDS

"When posing for a photo, always angle your
elbow out slightly so that the upper part of your
arm does not flatten out against your side."

—Rex Lott, fashion photographer

"Try not to have your picture taken with models. Even
if you're a fairly attractive person, you will always look a
little heavy and kind of homely next to them."

—Betty Sze, ex-model agent

*R*ampant picture taking is one of the greatest fat traps of family gatherings and special occasions. Heck, with the prevalence of fancy cell phones, you've practically got to be camera ready from the moment you wake up in the morning.

The other day on the subway I was wearing my New York uniform–black dress, enormous black sunglasses from cool-as-hell Australian designer Tsubi (the sunglasses make me look like a car), carrying an enormous black Comme des Garçons valise (a totally important designer label); yes, it's suitcaselike in proportion, but how else is a girl meant to carry spare stilettos in New York?) and listening to my iPod (white earbuds are still very chic).

It was around midday and there weren't that many people around. Sitting across from me was a mom and her two teenage sons. They obviously were tourists—they were wearing shorts and backpacks, had guidebooks, and were sporting cameras, the whole nine-mug-me-I'm-a-tourist yards.

A few minutes into the ride, the mom made one of her sons get up, walk over to me, and stand next to me while she snapped a picture. Then he went back to his seat and they giggled a little bit. All without saying a word to me.

The first thoughts that went through my mind immediately after I realized I had been camera-ambushed by rogue tourists were:

(1) I am not an animal in a zoo.
(2) Just because I have my sunglasses on doesn't mean I can't see you.
(3) Thank GOD I'm wearing contouring powder and lip gloss!!!!

There's probably nothing more demoralizing than dieting 24-7, putting on a pretty frock, and winding up looking chubby in photographs anyway.

For the first twenty-two years of my life, I bought into the conventional, defeatist mentality that teaches us that the camera instantly adds five pounds. Then, when I was signed to a plus-size modeling agency and started having my photos taken for money, I quickly learned there are some no-fail tricks you can employ to look thinner and more fabulous in front of the camera.

Here are my favorite tips on how to vamp it up for your very own money shot. If you practice, practice, practice in front of the mirror, you might get so good at them that you'll be plagued with the same problem as I have now—looking thinner in photos than you do in real life!

EXPERT TIP: "Working with teenage models who do not have a ton of experience, you see a lot of bad posture on set. Slouching in photographs will cause you took look curvy. I always use my experience as a ballet dancer to make the girls look slimmer. My ballet teacher always used to tell me, pretend you're 'pulling up your zipper'—keep your torso straight, your belly tucked in, buttocks firm, and hands at your side. It is the easiest way to look thin and elongated in photographs."
—Shane Cisneros, fashion editor

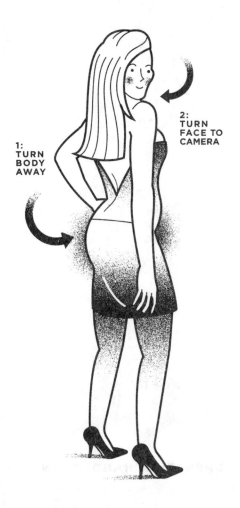

1:
TURN
BODY
AWAY

2:
TURN
FACE TO
CAMERA

TIP 1: THE TURN-AND-LOOK MANEUVER

To pull off this red-carpet favorite, turn your body almost entirely away from the camera and twist your head back around. Make sure to lower your chin and smile. Bingo! You're half the size you were before.

TIP 2: OPERATION HAND-ON-WAIST This trick works wonders on your waist by creating a space between your body and your arms, which, in turn, places emphasis on the curve of your waist and creates the illusion of a perfect hourglass figure. It works particularly well when combined with the aforementioned Turn-and-Look. From the back, you'll look almost as curvaceous as Jennifer Lopez!

TIP 3: THE THREE-QUARTER PROFILE TRICKEROO An industry favorite—most of my European fashion friends, both male and female, refuse to be photographed any other way. The Three-Quarter Profile, when done correctly, can create instant cheekbones as well as remove all traces of chin flab and big-nose-ness. It's easy and perfect for close-ups.

Turn your head slightly away from the camera, tilt your upper jaw up and point your chin down. Too tricky to combine with other moves, but excellent for the emergency sit-down photo.

TIP 4: THE HALF-TURN PIROUETTE If turning your body entirely away from the camera seems too
posey, a half-turn is a terrific second option. Make sure
you have one leg slightly closer to the camera with that
toe pointed directly at the lens. This creates a long, lean
look.

HOW NOT TO LOOK FAT

Stand up super-straight to avoid revealing your back fat. You might even want to try leaning ever so slightly backward from the hip to look taller and, ergo, thinner.

FOOLPROOF TIP: Totally caught off guard by a snap-happy friend? Hide your double chin in one second flat by pushing the back of your tongue up against your soft palate—that soft part in the back of the roof of your mouth. This tenses up the muscle under your jaw and minimizes chin flab hang-down.

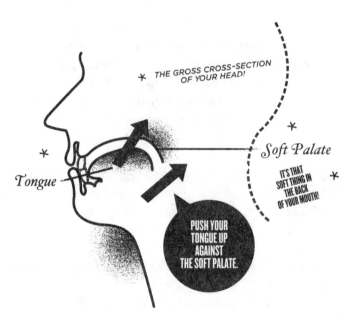

✳ THE GROSS CROSS-SECTION OF YOUR HEAD!

✳ Soft Palate

✳ Tongue

PUSH YOUR TONGUE UP AGAINST THE SOFT PALATE.

IT'S THAT SOFT THING IN THE BACK OF YOUR MOUTH! ✳

Chapter 25

INSIDE YOUR HEAD

"One thing to remember is the world
is full of chubby chasers. Try a holiday in Egypt or
Morocco to boost your morale; they love
fat women there."
**—Diane Pernet, fashion and video journalist,
AShadedViewonFashion.com**

*B*esides posing for photographs, there are very specific ways to carry yourself that will make you look slimmer nearly every moment of every day. It doesn't stop there, either.

Most women who think they are fat (need a serious injection of self-esteem, but that's besides the point) develop very particular behaviors and body movements—like slouching, standing with bent knees, splaying their hanging arms out to the side, leading with their stomachs when walking, and tucking the chin in and pitching the head and neck forward—that subconsciously scream to the outside world, "I'm fat! I think I'm fat! Fat fat fat!"

Stop it now; here's how.

Body Language

Ever notice how models carry themselves with a certain lanky grace? It's this body language, much of which is a cultivated by-product of hours and days of posing on photo shoots, that women of all sizes should learn to adopt. Instead of "I'm fat and I feel bad about my body," standing, walking, sitting, and moving with a contrived gazellelike grace will trick the outside world into believing your body is svelter than you imagine it to be.

HOW TO STAND BETTER: Watch people standing in line or waiting around on the street corner and you'll notice that people with bigger thighs tend to stand with their toes splayed outward—as if they are large ballerinas stuck, permanently, in first position.

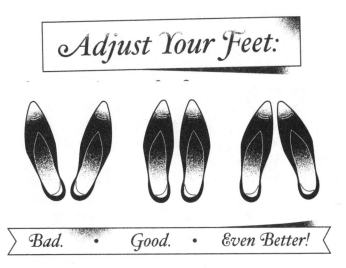

Adjust Your Feet:

Bad. • Good. • Even Better!

This is natural—and lazy. When the inner thighs are a bit bigger, it's easier to splay your toes outward, leaving your outer thigh muscles slack to accommodate their flaccid inner brethren.

But hang around backstage at a fashion show or at fashion schools (I recommend ones in London for seeing the coolest girls) and you'll find that skinny and not-so-skinny fashion girls stand either with their toes pointed straight forward or even ever-so-slightly pigeon-toed.

If you've ever admired the seductive curve of a runner's thigh, try standing by the same principle—turning your toes just that much inward tenses up your outer thigh, creating a leaner, sexier line, and also helps to de-emphasize any overabundance of inner thigh flesh.

HOW TO WALK BETTER: Here is something I learned, at an early age, from my mother, a thin person: When you walk, point your toes forward and pay special attention that your thighs brush against each other. Waddling down the street with toes and legs splayed wide apart looks clumsy, which, in turn, makes the whole individual look wider.

On the other end of the spectrum, see models catwalking—by placing one foot directly in front of the other in a heel-toe-heel-toe sequence, they appear even longer and leaner than they already are.

It's up to you to find a good balance between waddling and catwalking—to each her own center of gravity. Whatever you end up doing, stand up straight, square your shoulders, and go for it with confidence.

CATWALKING
FUN Y'ALL...

Watch models sashay down the runway, and you'll notice they place one foot directly in front of the other. Doing so creates a long, lean line and a sexy little swing in the hips that will make you look taller and slimmer.

HOW TO SIT BETTER: Remember when you were a child and your mother told you to sit up straight? Well, it's time to grow up and heed that advice because not only is it good for your back and innards (when you slouch your back strains and you're crushing your vital organs), but it will make you look taller and thinner.

As an addendum to your mom's advice: Take a page out of finishing-school decorum guidelines and practice pinning those knees together. It'll be hard at first, but it gets easier the more you try. And it's worth it. Following the same principle of standing with your toes pointed forward or slightly pigeon-toed, sitting with your knees splayed outward only shows off and emphasizes the girth of your inner thighs.

BODY DYSMORPHIA: A few years ago I participated in a *Marie Claire* magazine story. Setting aside any shred of dignity I had at the time, I voluntarily posed for photos in a silver bathing suit and allowed the features staff to morph my photos ten times over—making my thighs bigger in some pictures, chunking up my waist, adding pounds here and there. The challenge was, in the end, for me to pick my "real body" out of a lineup. I mistakenly picked a "fat" photo.

Fact is, most women—something like 90 percent of us!—suffer from mild cases of body dysmorphia—the belief that they are larger than they really are. It's a normal state of mind.

So be aware that however large you imagine yourself to be, you're 90 percent likely to not actually be that big.

That's all.

HOW NOT TO LOOK FAT

How to Love the Way You Look—
Your Self-Esteem

When I was writing my column for the *New York Post*, I drew a lot of ire from certain communities for freely using words like "fat," "chubby," and "chunky." Just because I wasn't hedging my semantics behind the safety of watered-down political correctness, some people took grave offense to my column and called it "rude" and "trash."

But here's the rub—it's time to get real.

Let's call a spade a spade.

All across the country, women wake up in the morning worried about how they look. So many people don't like the way their bodies feel—I've certainly looked in the mirror and called myself fat. We've all had days where we feel ugly. No use couching it behind diluted language.

No one can hand you self-esteem on a platter. It doesn't matter how many times people tell you you're gorgeous, you will pick and choose when and whether you believe them. Self-esteem is up to you to find within yourself.

Still, I believe that clothing is one of the few things that can make an instant change to our appearances. The right shirt, pants, skirt, and shoes can create virtual miracles. And even if you don't feel particularly good about the body you have underneath, you can feel great about the effort you've made and the way you present yourself to the world. That's one thing you can control right now. That's one thing you know you can feel good about.

APPENDIX: SHOPPING RESOURCES

Chapter 1: Underwear

Intimacy: myimacyofatlanta.com

Hanes Body Enhancer underwear: hanes.com

Hanky Panky underwear: shopbop.com

JCPenney: jcpenney.com

Rago Shapewear: ragoshapewear.com

Chapter 2: Tops

Bravissimo lingerie: bravissimo.com

Chapter 3: Jeans

Blue Cult: bluecult.com

Bravissimo: bravissimo.com

Earnest Sewn: earnestsewn.com

Intimacy: myintimacy.com

Kasil: kasiljean.com

Levi's: levi.com

Salt Works: shopbop.com

Chapter 6: Onesies
Designer Cheat Sheet for Ladies Size 14+

Bless: bless-service.de

Century 21: c21stores.com

Chanel: chanel.com

Chanel factory store: premiumoutlets.com

Christian Dior: dior.com

Christian Dior factory store: premiumoutlets.com

Comme des Garçons: (212) 604-9200

Thierry Mugler: thierrymugler.com

Y-3 Adidas: adidas.com/y-3

Yohji Yamamoto: yohjiyamamoto.co.jp

Yves Saint Laurent: ysl.com

Chapter 8: Shoes

Ann Demeulemeester: store info at barneys.com

Converse: converse.com

Doc Martens: drmartens.com

Gap: gap.com

Kenneth Cole: kennethcole.com

Nine West: ninewest.com

Payless Shoe Source: payless.com

Terry de Havilland: Terrydehavilland.com

UGG: uggaustralia.com

Chapter 9: Outerwear

Moncler: moncler.it

Chapter 10: Accessories

Agent Provocateur: agentprovocateur.com

American Apparel: americanapparelstore.com

Ann Demeulemeester: store info at barneys.com

BCBG: bcbg.com

Blue Cult jeans: bluecult.com

Bravissimo lingerie and clothing: bravissimo.com

Chanel: chanel.com

Christian Dior: dior.com

Club Monaco: clubmonaco.com

Cole Haan: colehaan.com

Constanca Basto shoes: (212) 645-3233

Converse: converse.com

Donna Karan hosiery: donnakaran.com

Eley Kishimoto: eleykishimoto.com; store info at barneys.com

Fantasie lingerie: fantasie.co.uk; figleaves.com; bravissimo.com; myintimacy.com

Frederic Fekkai: fredericfekkai.com

Freya lingerie: figleaves.com; bravissimo.com; myintimacy.com

Gap: gap.com

Gold Toe: goldtoe.com

Hanes Maximum Control Top Underwear: hanes.com

Hermès: hermes.com

H&M: hm.com

James Perse: jamesperse.com

Juicy Couture: juicycouture.com; shopbop.com

Kasil jeans: kasiljean.com

Lanvin: lanvin.com

Marks & Spencer: marksandspencer.com

Marina Rinaldi: store info at saks.com

Old Navy: oldnavy.com

Rago Shapewear: ragoshapewear.com

Reciproque: 88-123 rue de la Pompe, 75016 Paris, 011-33-1-47-04-30-28

Salt Works jeans: shopbop.com

Sergio Rossi: sergiorossi.com

Seven at Lane Bryant: lanebryant.com

Shin at Paul Labrecque Salon & Spa: paullabrecque.com

Spanx: spanx.com

Splendid: splendidtees.com

Tahari: elietahari.com

Wacoal lingerie: wacoal-america.com

Yves Saint Laurent: ysl.com

Chapter 11: Special Occasions

The Knot: theknot.com

Chapter 13: Swimwear

L.L. Bean: llbean.com

Milla swimwear: figleaves.com

Speedo: speedo.com

Venus Swimwear: venusswimwear.com

Chapter 16: Hair

Frederic Fekkai: fredericfekkai.com

Shin at Paul Labrecque Salon & Spa: paullabrecque.com

Chapter 17: Makeup

Maybelline New York: maybelline.com

Chapter 19: Spa Treatments

Anushka Day Spa: 502 Madison Avenue, New York City,
    (212) 355-6404, gkspa.com

Brazil Bronze: 580 Broadway, Suite 501, New York City,
    (212) 431-0077, brazilbronze.com

Completely Bare Spa: Various locations in New York,
    (212) 366-6060, completelybare.com

Dr. Denese: drdenese.co.uk

Chapter 20: Sleep Yourself Thinner

DuWop: duwop.com

MAC: maccosmetics.com

Chapter 22: Drinking

AER Club & Lounge: 409 West 13th Street,
New York City, (212) 989-0100, aerlounge.com

Bacardi Island Breeze: Bacardi.com

The Gym (on Madison Square Park): thegym.com

Lotus: 409 West 14th Street, New York City, (212) 243-
4420, lotusnewyork.com

The Sports Club/LA: thesportsclubla.com

Star Room: 378 Montauk Highway, Wainscott, NY,
(631) 537-3332

White Lie Early Season Chardonnay: whiteliewines.com

INDEX

Page numbers in *italics* refer to illustrations.